A PLOT
TO KILL

A PLOT
TO KILL

A True Story of Deception, Betrayal and Murder in a Quiet English Town

DAVID WILSON

sphere

SPHERE

First published in Great Britain in 2021 by Sphere

1 3 5 7 9 10 8 6 4 2

A CIP catalogue record for this book
is available from the British Library.

Hardback ISBN 978-0-7515-8216-1
Export ISBN 978-0-7515-8215-4

Typeset in Warnock by M Rules
Printed and bound in Great Britain by
Clays Ltd, Elcograf S.p.A.

Papers used by Sphere are from well-managed forests
and other responsible sources.

MIX
Paper from
responsible sources
FSC® C104740

Sphere
An imprint of
Little, Brown Book Group
Carmelite House
50 Victoria Embankment
London EC4Y 0DZ

An Hachette UK Company
www.hachette.co.uk

www.littlebrown.co.uk

A further consideration tells us that the adult's sense of self cannot have been the same from the beginning. It must have undergone a process of development, which understandably cannot be demonstrated, though it can be reconstructed with a fair degree of probability.

SIGMUND FREUD,
Civilisation and Its Discontents

Introduction

In the end, I had to choose between two houses. A narrow, three-storey Edwardian building in need of repairs, as well as a functioning toilet, on the High Street in Thame, or a small, detached Victorian cottage in Buckingham, situated almost at the top of a hill – and therefore rather grandly named Hillside – and just a few hundred yards from a pub called the Mitre.

The pub won.

I bought Hillside in 1989 and would live in that house until I got married. When we started a family soon afterwards, we moved to a village that wasn't too far away from the town. We didn't really want to leave Buckingham: the schools were good; I enjoyed socialising at the rugby club; and the small, private University of Buckingham (UB), where one of my old university tutors taught History, offered some welcome cultural diversion. More generally, we liked the people who live there.

It has a sense of community; it really was and remains a place where most people know one another.

Buckingham was also just a fifteen-minute drive from

HMP Grendon. That was the prison where I had just become a governor, and the reason why I had to choose between the house in Thame or Hillside. From then on, and for the rest of my prison career, I made certain that any other jails that I was posted to, such as HMP Woodhill in Milton Keynes, were all easily commutable from Buckingham.

I have now lived in or around the town for over thirty years.

A murder in a sleepy market town like Buckingham is unusual, but not unheard of – after all, people fall out with each other everywhere and all the time. Murders don't just happen on the 'troubled estates' of our inner cities, but can occur in isolated or busy English middle-class villages, on remote Scottish islands, in the Welsh mountains, or, frankly, anywhere that people come to live and interact with one another. The phenomenon of murder transcends place, class and ethnicity, although perhaps not gender. Murder really is a man's, and usually a young man's, business. Husbands kill wives and boyfriends kill girlfriends. All too often young men exchange angry words with other young men on a Friday night and, when their anger is a potent cocktail of too much alcohol, drugs and bravado, it can often lead to violence, and sadly sometimes to murder.

In my job as a prison governor, and now in my work as a criminologist, I'd hear stories like that all the time. Now usually much older, the teller would sit opposite me in my office and explain how they came to kill another human being. Most were ashamed of what they had done – although sometimes that was difficult to ascertain, as they were usually trying to convince me that they should be given parole and be released back into the community. No matter what they said, some were clearly dangerous, and a fair few still battling some inner demons, meaning their chances of being released were non-existent. As well as my more formal evaluations, I used to have a rule of thumb: would I want this man to be my next-door neighbour?

If I couldn't be certain of my answer I would err against parole.

Murder has been my business for all of my professional career and, as such, very little now shocks me. I've met notorious serial killers such as Dennis Nilsen who, prior to disposing of his victims, liked to prop up their bodies in a chair to have a conversation with them; teenage hitmen who were happy to take the life of another human being for as little as £200; and a mild-mannered family annihilator who murdered his wife and two children prior to burning down the house that they had shared for fifteen years. I am not surprised by what some men are capable of doing to the women and children they supposedly love, nor am I surprised by young men hurting other young men. My job is often to try to make sense of what at first appears to make no sense; to make the irrational and unusual explicable. Sometimes I can't and I'm left shaking my head, or shrugging my shoulders. Even as a humanist, having worked with some of our most notorious murderers and several serial murderers I have still occasionally felt that I was in the presence of evil.

And yet, I was astounded when I first heard about a murder that took place in Buckingham in 2015. Good old Buckingham! The place where my kids went to school and where I still enjoyed a pint in the Mitre. This murder was so extraordinary that at first I didn't believe what I was being told, and wondered whether the story had simply been exaggerated.

What was that? Peter Farquhar, the Head of English at Stowe School? Oh, the ex-head. Didn't he lecture at the university? Murdered! By one of his students, Benjamin Field. Was this the same rather serious and religious Ben Field who worked part-time in a local nursing home, taught at the university, became a warden at Stowe Parish Church, and whose father was a minister? The same Ben and Peter who had solemnised their love for one another in a betrothal ceremony in 2014, even though there were forty years between them!

Are you certain?

Yes.

The victim and the perpetrator could easily have been my neighbours.

These were the basic details, but I would later discover there was much more to this extraordinary story. This was no spontaneous murder, the result of two young men falling out with each other on a Friday night; it was cross-generational and committed by what criminologists call a 'process-focused' perpetrator. Killers like Colin Ireland, who liked to slowly torture his victims prior to murdering them, or the nurse Beverly Allitt, who enjoyed the spectacle of the emergencies that she created on the children's ward where she worked and killed. They didn't want death to come immediately, but over time. Ben Field took his time too, and over the course of five years gradually groomed Peter and the local community in which he lived, to enable him to get away with murder. So successful was Field's grooming, he had become secretary to the parochial church council in September 2014, and was confirmed at Stowe Parish Church in 2015. At the university, he had become their 'poster boy' – he conducted undergraduate seminars and his masters dissertation was published by the university press.

Astoundingly, when he was on bail for murdering Peter, Field even preached a sermon at his father's church on the theme of 'Thou Shalt Not Kill'.

As I looked more deeply into the case I'd discover still more extraordinary details about the murder that took me to the dark heart of 'Middle England' and the solid, seemingly dependable institutions that keep it propped up – school, university, church and various state-funded organisations such as the police, the Coroner's Service and the NHS.

I became aware that people were desperately keen to talk about the murder with me but, at the same time, to be seen to have said absolutely nothing at all; they wanted to be close to what had happened but distanced too. Buckingham reacted with sensation, but also with what passed as silence. Of course, there was an understandable and heartfelt shock about what had happened to Peter, but there was also an almost universal failure to acknowledge that this murder had taken place under our noses – in plain sight – in our close-knit community. If we were honest with ourselves, we'd done nothing to stop it from happening.

I was intrigued by this murder, but I was also initially reluctant to write about the case. I had just finished a book about a murder in a Scottish town called Carluke, where I had grown up, which had taken place in 1973. I knew from researching that book – *Signs of Murder* – that I needed to ask people, often family members and friends, some difficult and often intrusive questions, and that raking over these historical coals could easily cause distress or annoyance. There are always sensitivities that need to be remembered when discussing murder – even a murder that occurred almost half a century ago. It had been difficult for me in Carluke to talk about a murder that had happened in 1973 and so I suspected that there would be more immediate problems with this case by asking the same types of questions in the community that was now my home and about a murder that was still fresh in the memory.

Ultimately, I came to realise that I was actually asking the same question about both of these cases. Who was responsible for the murder?

From the very outset, I detected that some people felt everything that had happened had simply been Peter's 'business' – by which they meant it was his fault he'd been killed.

After all, it was Peter, they reasoned, who had invited a much younger man to live in his home. Later on, when it became abundantly clear that all was not right with their relationship, Peter had nonetheless remained loyal to his younger partner. Why had Peter not done something when it was obvious, at least from the outside, that the relationship was failing? Wasn't it inevitable that a young man couldn't live with an older partner? This wasn't 'normal', as one person explained it to me. Peter should have kicked Field out of his house and got on with his life.

This is a subtle form of victim-blaming, masked by the politest of concern, all wrapped up in the self-serving belief that they'd been respecting other people's privacy. It seemed to me like weaponised gentility.

The more I looked into the case, the more convinced I became that Buckingham had also been lucky. If Peter's failure to act was due to Field's skill as a perpetrator, then the town could easily have been dealing with a serial killer. Field had very nearly got away with Peter's murder, and it would appear that, had all of his plans come to fruition, Peter would have been the first in a long list of elderly victims.

People are always surprised when I tell them that the elderly are the group most targeted by British serial killers. Murderers like Kenneth Erskine, Patrick Mackay, Stephen Akinmurele and, of course, Harold Shipman all preferred to kill older people. Shipman was a trusted local GP who killed 215 – and perhaps as many as 260 – of his overwhelmingly elderly patients and used his singleton practice and home visits to gain access to his victims. The practice of medicine had allowed him to kill and it seemed to me that Field had used his supposed faith and the practice of religion in a similar way.

To what extent, I also wondered, was the distancing from what had happened to Peter also about our own fear of growing old and then dying? We all know that we will one day die, but choose not to talk about it. We accept on some subconscious level that we are all mortal, but we put off any discussion about what that might mean both practically and philosophically, because it is just too hard to face. So we distance ourselves from that reality and, as a consequence, our inevitable mortality is rarely discussed. Life is for living, not for being morbid. This seems to be the preferred approach, at least until it's too late to do anything else.

When people spoke to me about Peter's murder, they seemed fascinated by the case, and yet also uncomfortable talking about death. How, I wondered, do these widespread cultural fears and anxieties about our own mortality coexist with our continuing fascination with murder and serial killers?

This awful case had started to make me think very deeply about the town I was happy to call my home.

Bit by bit, I realised that I did want to write about Peter's murder, but there was a problem. Although I had met Peter in the past, and had occasionally spoken to him, I did not know him. I wondered how I could bring his story to life, beyond the various things that had previously been written or broadcast about the case. Where would I even start? In a small community like Buckingham, I could of course easily speak to people who knew Peter – and my personal connections in the town would certainly help. I thought about approaching Peter's surviving family members, but I decided against this avowedly biographical methodology. It hardly seemed to capture all of what had happened and, in any event, various materials had been published in the wake of Peter's murder that helped me to reconstruct a picture of his life without having to intrude on his surviving family's privacy.

I also wrote a couple of letters to Field, having located the prisons where he was on remand and then where he had been sent after his conviction, in the hope of starting a correspondence.

In the end, it was a chance encounter with a friend that helped me to choose where to begin my research. She knew Peter, and had even attended the book club he hosted on several occasions; she reminded me that Peter had left three self-published novels. I will freely admit to being no literary scholar, but these books became the starting point of my research and the platform on which to build my narrative. They would prove invaluable in allowing me to understand the various issues that had come to pattern Peter's life, his struggle with his faith and sexuality, and how he was particularly vulnerable to Field's grooming.

But there was more.

While reading one of these novels, I was struck by how the events in the book seemed to echo the way in which Peter would eventually die. He seemed to be speaking to me from beyond the grave, offering valuable clues about his murder.

*

As my research continued, I came to realise that this case has implications for us all. It is not just about a murder and a potential serial killer; it's also about how communities look out for each other, or fail to do so. It offers us a way to discuss growing old, dying and death in a culture that is obsessed with youth, and how the old and the young can live together, rather than being kept apart. Perhaps most important of all, it also gives us an opportunity to reflect on what it means to live an authentic life. My research and writing during a global pandemic seemed to heighten the importance of these disparate threads that would entwine to tell Peter's story.

That seems like a lot for even the story of an extraordinary murder to hold, but as I tried to make sense of what had happened it struck me that the context for understanding Peter's death was to grasp the very essence of what it means to live.

CHAPTER ONE

Lest We Forget

'Like something out of a novel'

CROWN PROSECUTION SERVICE

On the morning of Monday 26 October 2015, Peter Anthony Scott Farquhar was found dead in his house at 3 Manor Park in Maids Moreton, on the edge of Buckingham. His cleaner found his body slumped on the sofa in the living room, which was situated just to the right of the front door, opposite a downstairs toilet. There was a near-empty bottle of Aberlour whisky on the table beside the sofa. The room looked messy, disordered and in need of a good tidy-up; it really did require the services of a cleaner. Judge that observation for yourself, as everything that morning was captured by the body camera of the female police officer who responded to the cleaner's call, and which would later be shown in the Channel 4 documentary *Catching a Killer: A Diary from the Grave*.

For a few fleeting and distressing frames, we even catch a glimpse of Peter's lifeless body.

A doctor was called, and then, because the cause of death was unknown, so too was the coroner – the judicial officer tasked with finding out what had happened. In this case it was Richard Hulett, the chief coroner for Buckinghamshire. Hulett was a lawyer by training and had presided over thirty thousand deaths since being appointed in 1991. He was just a few months away from retiring and in an interview that he gave to a local paper said that he was looking forward to travelling around Europe, without having to 'worry about rushing back, or being able to fit in the travel'. I'm not certain how to interpret that statement, but Hulett duly arranged for an inquest to be held in Beaconsfield, in the south of the county, in November 2015, and ruled that Peter had died of 'acute alcohol intoxication', as 'a result of an accident'.

Case closed. Move along now – nothing to see here.

Like the good people of Middle England that we all are, that's more or less what we did.

Perhaps if you had known Peter, you might be tempted to call his life ordinary, but it hadn't been uneventful. He had been a very successful Head of English at one of England's most famous public schools, a lecturer in English literature at the University of Buckingham, and had (self)-published three novels: *Between Boy and Man* (2010), *A Bitter Heart* (2012) and *A Wide Wide Sea* (2015). These were all noteworthy achievements rather than run-of-the-mill, but it was the circumstances in which he was killed that would make him extraordinary. When the truth surrounding Peter's death finally came to light, the Crown Prosecution Service described the case as 'like something out of a novel'.

The CPS is not noted for irony.

In fact, it had been a love of literature that had brought Peter and his killer together.

Literature had been a constant in Peter's life, whether as a student, teacher or author. His favourite book, I was told during my research, was *The Ambassadors* by Henry James and, for over a decade, he had run a very serious book club in Buckingham. The Stowe Reading Group (sometimes also known as Stowe Reading Circle) met three times a year and how that group was organised and what was discussed there offers us glimpses of 'literary Peter' that can help us to understand how he went about writing, and what it was he chose to write about.

Peter was sixty-nine years old when he died, but I am uncertain if I should describe him as elderly. Where elderly begins seems to be different for everyone, or is sometimes simply linked to the age at which we retire. There are about 285 people aged sixty-five and over, the typical age of retirement, for every thousand people aged sixteen to sixty-four in the UK. We seem to be much more interested in this latter group, the 'working age' population. We debate endlessly about the taxes they pay, the interests they have and where, and on what, they might want to spend their hard-earned cash. We know about the cars they drive, the books they read and the TV programmes they like to watch. Their world is envied, visible and seemingly vital, not just because we think it's important, but because we consciously choose not to discuss anything else.

By contrast, we don't really know that much about the lives of the elderly, even if we all recognise that the population is living longer. Unless something dramatic happens to make them visible – like, most recently, COVID-19 – the elderly are unseen and voiceless; they are the 'walking dead', all too often shut off in residential care homes to await the inevitable. At the height of the first wave of the pandemic, nearly four hundred people died in care homes every day, partly because patients were, inexplicably, discharged from hospital to these homes without COVID-19 tests, exposing other residents to the virus. The Office for National Statistics (ONS) suggested that, by June 2020, of all the people who had died as a result of COVID-19, four in five were aged seventy or over. As we grow old we are, of course, more prone to illness, but I can't help but wonder whether the invisibility of the elderly more generally contributed to this statistic. The ONS also noted that older people were more likely to experience feelings of isolation, depression and helplessness as a result of the various lockdown measures introduced by the government.

COVID-19 had shown us, rather starkly, how easy it is to forget about the elderly and regard them as expendable. But this is neither natural nor inevitable; rather, it is the result of conscious choices that we make as a culture. So too elder abuse is more common than we might expect, partly because we choose not to discuss it and the elderly are much more likely to be victims of fraud, financial scams, violence or, in extreme cases, murder or serial murder.

Sadly, no matter his achievements, it was Peter's murder that made him visible, although it would be some time before we could see most of the details clearly. Some of those details are still, despite my best efforts, impossible to establish.

So astonishing were the issues surrounding his death, Peter's murder inspired not only *Catching a Killer: A Diary from the Grave* but also a Radio 5 Live special called *Killer in the Congregation* and, as I write, there has been an announcement that the BBC has commissioned a drama about the case, to be called *The Sixth Commandment*. However, the two documentaries never really offered much insight into what might have motivated Peter's killer, preferring to concentrate on the police investigation to catch him, or the reactions of his former school friends and acquaintances to his conviction for murder. We didn't really learn anything about Buckingham or Maids Moreton either. Even the pictures used in the Channel 4 documentary of a village green and a quaint church were of a totally different place – perhaps it was easier to film there than in Maids Moreton.

For me, this is not good enough. I want to go further; much further.

I want to understand the killer's psychology and why, having got away with one murder, he seems to have been prepared to take steps towards another and, by doing so, increased the chances of being unmasked. And, if he had succeeded in killing another, just how many others would he have killed? How was he able to seduce so many people and in such intimate spaces like a church, a university and the town of Buckingham – spaces where, to put it mildly, everyone knows everyone else's business? How did living and worshipping in Buckingham and studying English literature at the local university shape the mechanics of the murder?

After the murder had been committed and Field was convicted, there was a tendency to make him responsible for everything that had happened, and to reclaim Peter for the undisturbed status quo of Middle England. This did not reflect what had really happened at all. More worryingly, several of the institutions that Field had used to serve his murderous purpose didn't seem to want to reflect on what had happened, and how a killer had become central to their culture. They seem to prefer to hide their heads in the sand, without realising that if they don't take steps to change there's nothing to stop another killer from doing exactly the same. I remain convinced that Field could easily have become one of our most notorious and prolific serial killers, and that what happened in Maids Moreton could just as easily still happen again.

Criminologically speaking, a serial killer is someone who kills three or more victims in a period of greater than thirty days; so there is a numeric threshold in terms of the number of victims before this label can be applied, and also an element of time. The serial killer does not kill his victims all at once, but in a period of greater than thirty days. Killing over time allows the serial killer to savour and then perfect their deadly business. Taking the lives of other people in this process-focused manner makes the killer feel powerful and omnipotent – in their own minds, they are God-like.

Our most prolific serial killer (and one of the world's most deadly) remains Harold Shipman, who killed over two hundred of his patients, starting with his first victim, Eva Lyons, in March 1975, and murdering his final victim – Kathleen Grundy – in June 1998. Shipman was murdering for over two decades, and was able to do so because he had groomed the community of Hyde in Manchester. They liked to think of him as a trusted, old-fashioned local GP who was prepared to undertake home visits to see his often elderly patients. Having this sort of access merely allowed Shipman to decide who should live and who should die, and no one was prepared to talk about the suspicious nature of these sudden deaths and challenge the word of a doctor. Like Peter, many of Shipman's victims were found slumped in a chair, or on the sofa, seemingly having slipped away in their sleep, despite the fact that they had often been in good health before their doctor had come calling. In the same way that Peter's body had to be exhumed to discover the truth about his death, so too were the bodies of several of Shipman's victims. Only then was it established that they died from overdoses of morphine, as opposed to natural causes.

Field similarly used all the tools at his disposal to gain access to his victims: he worked in a care home; he became respected within the university; and he was trying to become a priest. That last prospect should make us all pause and reflect. It should especially make the Church of England (and other denominations too) think very carefully about the lessons that must be learnt from this case, particularly about those Christians who are gay. What safeguarding has the Church of England put in place following Field's conviction, to stop this type of murder from happening again, and how rigorous is their vetting of those who want to become priests? If the answer to this latter question is 'not very', could there be others now preaching who have evil designs on their parishioners?

Grooming is something which we tend to think of adults doing to children, rather than a process that the (relatively) young can sometimes do to the elderly, or indeed a phenomenon that can happen to a community as a whole. Just as Shipman groomed the town of Hyde to think of him as a reliable GP, Field had groomed Buckingham to consider him a serious scholar and a committed Christian. That grooming gave him the access to the victims he needed to become a serial killer; Field had even written a hit-list of elderly people he seemingly would have gone on to target after Peter. It included his own parents, other members of his family and elderly people that he encountered from his work and association with the university. I'm sure, if he hadn't been stopped, he would have slowly made his way down that list, perfecting the way he killed and, like Shipman, enjoying his perverted power to do as he pleased – perhaps for decades.

To successfully groom an individual, an institution or a community, the perpetrator needs to get close. It takes skill and a certain amount of cunning and intellect. The perpetrator needs to understand what makes those institutions, communities or individuals tick, so that they can say and do the right things, or behave in a way that creates a sense of connection. To fit in, they need to be good actors, because they secretly want to stand out.

Peter had taught English literature to Field at university, and it was through this bond, their shared love of literature, that their relationship would begin to take shape. As I continued my research, I started to see strange similarities between the novels that Field had studied and the events that took place in real life. Peter was also a writer, and so his writing gives us an insight into who he was as an individual and the issues which came to preoccupy his mind. Field even helped to edit one of Peter's novels, later on in their relationship. Again, on reading one of Peter's books, I noticed that the events in the novel eerily echoed those in Maids Moreton to the extent that they were like a blueprint for the murder. The line between fact and fiction was becoming well and truly blurred.

I am not suggesting a makeshift cause and effect, but I am convinced that this literary context allows us to understand the basis of their relationship, how that relationship started and then developed, offers an insight into Field's underlying personality, and finally reveals something about how the murder was actually committed. Themes within the novels seemed to have prompted action, and Field appeared to very consciously ape several of the more deadly characters whom he had encountered within his degree.

I don't think this proposition is so outlandish, and I will explain why.

We have all become used to the idea that TV programmes or movies 'cause' crimes through, for example, perpetrators engaging in copycat behaviour. Real life, including some actual murders, can be and sometimes is prompted, inspired and shaped by fantasy and fiction. Mark Twitchell, for example, was so obsessed with the TV series *Dexter* that he was inspired to murder John Altinger in 2008, and helpfully for the police investigation, he left various documents on his laptop explaining why. John Hinckley became so completely fixated with Martin Scorsese's *Taxi Driver*, and especially with Jodie Foster, that he moved to New Haven, Connecticut, so that he could stalk her while she was studying at Yale University and, motivated by the film's main character, who plots to kill a presidential candidate, Hinckley attempted to assassinate Ronald Reagan. In Britain, Stanley Kubrick's ultra-violent *A Clockwork Orange* had to be withdrawn from circulation after its release in 1971, given the number of crimes – including at least one murder – that were committed and which copied aspects of the film.

Some books have had a similar impact.

John Lennon's murderer, Mark Chapman, was obsessed with J. D. Salinger's *The Catcher in the Rye* and was clutching a copy of the book at the time of his arrest. He signed his police statement 'Holden Caulfield' – the protagonist in Salinger's novel. *The Turner Diaries*, a 1978 novel by William Luther Pierce, but published under the pseudonym Andrew Macdonald, depicts a violent revolution in the United States which leads to the overthrow of the government, a race war and the systematic extermination of people of colour. The book has inspired various right-wing terrorists, including: Timothy McVeigh, who was convicted and later executed for his part in the Oklahoma City bombing in 1995 (he had pages of the novel in his possession when he was arrested); David Copeland, a British neo-Nazi responsible for a bombing campaign in 1999 against London's black, Asian and gay communities and which resulted in three deaths – he quoted *The Turner Diaries* in his interviews with the police; and the Norwegian mass-murderer Anders Breivik, whose 'manifesto' was plagiarised from a number of sources, including *The Turner Diaries*. We could add to this murder-inspiring list *The Secret Agent* by Joseph Conrad, *The Queen of the Damned* by Anne Rice and *The Collector* by John Fowles.

This is not a new, or even recent, phenomenon. The American actor John Wilkes Booth, for example, had been so immersed in the plays of Shakespeare since his childhood, especially *Julius Caesar* – he was known for playing the role of Brutus – that his contemporaries speculated whether he had assassinated President Lincoln because Booth had lost his identity and that he was in some way re-enacting that role in reality. Brutus is of course one of Shakespeare's celebrated assassins and it may well be that Booth, a well-known Confederate sympathiser, hoped that he too would be honoured after Lincoln's death.

Booth had very little formal education and learned what he knew of Shakespeare through acting and the work of his actor father. This informal rather than institutional exposure led to him committing perhaps the most famous assassination in history. So, in the more rarefied, formalised environment of a university, where students are expected to immerse themselves in the texts they study, it hardly seems controversial to propose that the literature that a student encounters can have a similar effect.

*

At its heart, this is a book about a murder and a perpetrator who is likely to be a psychopath and was labelled as such at his trial, and who is suspected by the police of having wanted to kill many more older people. More broadly, it also uses the story of Peter Farquhar to examine what it means to be elderly in the UK and the lazy clichés that quickly get attached to old age.

A trope, for example, that the press set running after it became clear that Peter had been murdered, almost as if it was explanation enough, was that he was lonely. I really don't know how to measure loneliness or judge if that analysis is correct, but I certainly spoke with several individuals who knew him well and who felt that Peter's life had been very 'full' and 'fulfilling'. He had a group of friends and several outside interests, which included regular trips to Oxford and further afield to London to visit galleries and attend concerts. Peter was a creative man and, of course, writers often have to be solitary, but that is an entirely different experience from being lonely (as I can attest). We also know that, three times a year, Peter ran the Stowe Reading Group, where he would be surrounded by a circle of friends and acquaintances.

I'm not convinced that we can use loneliness as an explanation for Peter's gothic fate. Perhaps it's just what we like to tell ourselves to make us feel less culpable. It's the excuse that we think absolves us from failing to intervene when, at least at a common-sense level, what we see happening doesn't seem to make any sense; when we know that something isn't quite right.

But how do we make sense of murder, and should we turn to politics, religion, psychology or culture for an answer? A few people that I met in Buckingham had their own theories, but more generally they struggled just as much as everyone else to come to terms with what had happened in Maids Moreton and what this might 'mean' more broadly. I also became aware that it was often hard to escape informal conversations (if I had wanted to) about the murder. Quite apart from the formal interviews that I conducted, people wanted to discuss Peter's death, and the subsequent media interest in the case with me informally in the post office, at the checkout in Waitrose – where Trish Cowley, especially, would ask me about my research – or in the various cafés, restaurants, or pubs that allow people to gather in the town. Indeed I was usually asked 'When are you going to write about the Maids Moreton murder?', 'What was that all about, then?' 'He seemed like such a nice young man', or 'Can you believe that it happened here?' The answer, at least to that last question, is simple: yes I can; murder doesn't just happen somewhere else and murderers are often described as 'nice young men'.

Later I wondered whether the statement that 'it' had 'happened here' was also a comment about death. 'It' always surprises us as something unexpected, as something that happens to other people who live somewhere else; not to us, not here, despite all the evidence to the contrary.

*

There are many ways of telling a story, especially a story about a murder.

An obvious and popular method is to follow the police case in minute detail, with each twist and turn carefully considered. This is something which we have come to know as the police procedural. The danger is that all too often the police come to be viewed as the story, and editorially as a 'thin blue line': our noble – if sometimes flawed – capable, dogged guardians who keep the monsters at bay.

On the other hand, we might tell the story of the murder from the perspective of the killer, and what might have motivated him (and it usually is a him). I tend to favour this latter approach, but with a twist. I am conscious that telling a story in this way tends to obscure the life of the person who was killed. That's a real hazard, as the narrative often becomes centred on the killer, as opposed to the victim. I have never favoured that, either in my academic or my more popular writing, so instead have adopted what is sometimes called a victim-centred methodology. In other words, as far as this story is concerned, I want Peter to be front and centre, rather than his killer.

I want to bring Peter back to life, as it were, so that we hear his voice and become aware of what it is that he's trying to tell us. So I want to tell Peter's story using his writing and also delving into some of the books he taught or was especially fond of. However, there are dangers here too: inevitably, if my reading of Peter's final book *A Bitter Heart* is correct, we must relive the murder that took place. But perhaps this time, even if we can't save poor Peter, we might at least begin to understand how to prevent similar murders happening in the future.

To do all of this we need to look forwards, as well as back to the past and to the murder itself. 'Lest we forget.' It's the phrase commonly used in remembrance services, and first appeared in a poem by Rudyard Kipling. I don't want to forget Peter, but I also want our remembering of him and what happened to him to be as much about the future as it is about the history of this dreadful crime.

Adopting this methodology is also a way of trying to write about the murder honestly. As I continued with my research, I became acutely aware that after his death some institutions wanted to reclaim Peter as one of their own, while there was a parallel process of disowning Field. If only it were that easy. That reclaiming did not accurately reflect who Peter was as a man, and the speed with which Field was disowned did not capture how embedded he had become within the church, or at the university. If we want to learn the lessons of this murder, we have to be honest about why it occurred, where it took place, Field's personality, Peter's sexuality and faith, and why he was so easily seduced by Field. No matter how embarrassing it is now, we have to understand how Field became so entrenched at the university, and also a deputy warden at Stowe Parish Church.

Finally we need to consider geography.

This is a murder that really did take place in Middle England – Buckingham itself is often described as the 'pivot at the green heart of the country'. In the first few days and weeks of reporting the murder, the print and broadcast media especially had an irresistible urge to evoke the popular TV series *Midsomer Murders*. 'Middle England' therefore has a place in this story both metaphorically as well as geographically. Inevitably, class will rear its head. These are important issues, but if they come to dominate the narrative they only demean, rather than explain, this murder.

In choosing to set out on this journey I soon became aware that the story that I needed to tell was not just about making sense of an individual murder that took place in a somewhat privileged locale, or even of the interests that Peter had when he was alive. Of course these issues have their place, but I see in Peter's death more than all of this too. Join me on that journey, but I am not just going to write about a single murder, as I want to see the wood as much as the trees. For me the significance of this murder – what it 'means' – transcends place and raises broader issues about religion, gerontology, psychopathy, criminology, what it means to be elderly in this country and, perhaps most surprising of all, the insights that can be provided by a love of literature. Those are the contours of the forest that we are about to enter.

CHAPTER TWO

Peter Farquhar

'... sensual pleasure and altruism must, of
necessity be incompatible'

PETER FARQUHAR,
Between Boy and Man

I found a seat in the University of Buckingham's (UB) small
but efficient library, and took a pen and some paper out of
my rucksack, which I then hung on the back of my chair before
sitting down. I put the book that the librarian had found for
me on the table, opened it up and started to slowly begin the
process of taking notes – scribbling down names and snatches
of dialogue that seemed particularly important, and occasionally having to get out of my chair to track down some obscure
quotation in the text.

Time seemed to steal past me unobtrusively, and it was dark
before I eventually left the library.

I had decided to start my research by reading Peter's books.
I managed to track down copies of the first two novels, which

were self-published via AuthorHouse in Milton Keynes. As late as 2020, these two books were still for sale on their website. On the website's 'about the author' section, after outlining his teaching experience at Manchester Grammar School and Stowe, Peter was described as currently lecturing at the University of Buckingham.

He had actually been dead for five years.

Between Boy and Man was not Peter's first novel, but it was the first to be published, in 2010, some six years after he had retired from teaching at Stowe.

It was not well received, especially at Stowe.

Peter had been born in Edinburgh in 1946, and had a younger brother called Ian. Their father was a doctor, who later moved the family to London where Peter would be educated at Latymer Upper School in Hammersmith, before going on to Cambridge University. It is clear that throughout his novels he used autobiographical material about his life, his interests and the institutions he experienced. His novels are not about fantasy, escapism or the make-believe worlds of science fiction. The realism of his fiction might have been more about cream teas, classrooms and Christianity than the kitchen sink, but it was realism nonetheless. Above all else, his writing was personal; he was writing about his life. He therefore wrote about Cambridge University, where he had been awarded a First in English and had attended Churchill College; about his teaching experiences at Manchester Grammar, where he had worked between 1970 and 1982, and at Stowe, where he was made Head of English in 1989. His last novel, *A Bitter Heart,* draws on his experiences at UB and of teaching undergraduates, although it is set in Manchester.

All three novels also deal with the more intimate, moral dilemmas which Peter clearly struggled with, most obviously the tension between his Christianity and his sexuality. Put simply, could he have gay relationships and still retain his faith? He never seemed to be able to answer that question satisfactorily, either in his novels or in real life. There is a great deal of sermonising in his writing, and various characters are offered different platforms to talk about God, the meaning of life, guilt, forgiveness and sin. The books are infused with more secular dilemmas too. *Between Boy and Man* is very good at describing, for example, the tension between those who were attracted to the vocation of teaching, and how that idealism increasingly rubbed up against the changing culture of English public schools. Those changes meant that such schools were becoming less concerned with the development of individual students and much more with the need to make money in, as it was described to me by one teacher, 'a challenging market'.

The old 'chalk and talk' and nurturing approach to teaching was being replaced by computerised systems of monitoring and assessment, and of managerial practice more generally, which would not have been out of place in a shop, a bank or a factory. Peter neither liked these changes nor did he want to adapt to them.

Of course, every novelist draws on personal experience, but there appears to be much more than that in Peter's writing. He quite consciously uses the printed page to outline and then try to resolve issues and quandaries in his life; he could more effectively achieve this on paper than in reality. Peter writes to create order out of the especially chaotic and

28

messy psychological undertow of his personality and sexuality, even if the faithful, erudite face that he presented to the world showed little – if anything – of that private reality. His writing, at least until *A Bitter Heart*, shielded him from the practical consequences of being gay, although it is hard to escape the conclusion that both in his writing and in his life he was always desperate to give his love to someone. The tragedy of Peter's sexuality was that he was simply born in the wrong era, when homosexuality was still against the law – and then even when it became legal, he was oppressed by the official stance of the Church of England, which continued its intolerance towards homosexuality.

*

The title *Between Boy and Man* is a quotation from *Twelfth Night*: 'Not yet old enough for a man, nor young enough for a boy; as a squash is before 'tis a peascod, or a codling when 'tis almost an apple. 'Tis with him in standing water, between boy and man.' The novel is set in a boarding school called Moreton College which Peter clearly places in Buckingham (the characters even go for a drink in the Wheatsheaf – the name of a local pub). It opens with a death, when one of the key characters commits suicide by jumping in front of a train – Peter would also use a similar dramatic opening in *A Bitter Heart* – and follows the fortunes of three main characters: the Reverend John Donaldson, the school's chaplain, who also coaches the boys' football team; Jude Williams, a sixth-form pupil who is the star player in the team; and Alexander Scott, the Head of English.

The novel is 439 pages long, divided into thirty-three chapters and, at times, cloying and self-indulgent. Overly long, it is in want of a good editor. These criticisms notwithstanding, it paints an authentic picture of the close-knit world of boarding schools, where minor slights can quickly escalate into major issues, and of the various layers and underlying tensions between staff, management and pupils; the school and the community in which it is located; and between parents and teachers. It almost perfectly captures the often insane culture surrounding the Oxbridge interview; has a good ear for dialogue; and has a moral question that prompts the overall narrative – do sensual pleasures and altruism have to be incompatible? This question is sort-of answered in several ways, but we are left in no doubt that Christian faith is the best way to frame what that answer might be. Even so, it's hard to escape the feeling that Peter's writing reveals a more promiscuous nature even if, in the end, he settled for being a puritan for most of his life.

There are hints of Alan Bennett's play *The History Boys*, which opened at the National Theatre in 2004 and was later made into a successful film. While the play is set in a Sheffield grammar school rather than a boarding school in the Home Counties, a number of Bennett's themes are echoed in Peter's novel – most obviously like *The History Boys*, *Between Boy and Man* has an openly homoerotic sub-plot.

In a fit of pique at having been dropped from the football team, Jude claims that the Reverend Donaldson has sexually assaulted him. Jude is described as being 5′ 7″ and of a slight build, though with a neat, muscular body. He has a handsome face, with a 'fine bone structure and unexpectedly heavy, careless stubble. He had hazel eyes and light brown hair, cut conventionally short.' The reader is given enough information about the chaplain to know that, while this allegation might be false, Donaldson is indeed gay and does fantasise about young boys, especially Jude, and other members of staff. However, we are left in no doubt that he never acted upon these fantasies, and that Jude is simply making up the allegation to exact his revenge.

Peter is very good at creating a believable relationship between Jude and Donaldson that is important to both characters. For example, Jude says to the chaplain that he is 'special in my life. Not only are you one of my best mates, you are my mentor, my top advisor, perhaps even the father that I don't have.' A mate, a mentor, an advisor and a father are a heady mix of roles, but one is lacking: lover. It is tempting to see Peter's subsequent relationship with Field as one which, at last, fulfilled all of these roles. It should be emphasised that I never encountered any allegation of sexual impropriety about Peter during my research. One former pupil, the journalist and novelist George Pendle, who had often been invited to Peter's home in Maids Moreton for spaghetti Bolognese with some of his contemporaries, remembered that 'there were insinuations. He was, after all, an older unmarried man', but that he and his classmates merely 'classified Farquhar as a non-sexual being, like our parents'.

I won't spoil the ending of the novel, but what is more interesting than the novel's general story is how the book really does tell us something about Peter. The narrative not only gives us great insight into Peter's sexuality and how he attempted to reconcile it with his faith, but also tells us about his love of literature, and how the way that he taught was no longer fashionable in schools such as Stowe. That's the very quandary being described for Alexander Scott – Moreton College's Head of English.

Scott (one of Peter's middle names, and an obvious allusion to where he had been born) was 'an old timer', not in favour of the various managerial and technological changes that had been introduced at the school. It wasn't the changes in themselves that he disliked, although these were bad enough, but what they seemed to signify about teaching young people to love literature. Scott, who had a First in English from Cambridge (sound familiar?), is described as 'one of the cleverest men in the common room [and] widely regarded as one of the most brilliant Heads of English in the country'. It must have given Peter a great deal of satisfaction to have written that line. He was also described as being 'very caustic' and that 'Mr Scott's lashing tongue was famed throughout the College'. However, because of the changes being introduced at the school, Scott realised that there would be 'no place for him in the teaching of the future. Two years to retirement: not before time, if so much that he valued most was to be discarded.' There is also an echo here of Hector in *The History Boys* – an inspirational teacher, but whose teaching style (for various reasons) no longer fits with the ambitions of the headmaster.

Alexander Scott is clearly Peter Farquhar. Should anyone be in doubt, the obituary written by one of Peter's former pupils, the journalist and broadcaster Michael Crick, could have been taken directly from the pages of *Between Boy and Man*. Like all good obituaries, it was clearly written after discussion about Peter's life with his family, colleagues and friends; it was published in the *Guardian* on 18 November 2015. Crick, who stated that few people would ever forget Peter, described how he was slight and 'bird-like in appearance', but that he could not be taken advantage of – as many pupils found to their cost. In particular, Peter could be 'withering' – a polite way of saying cutting and sarcastic – in response to a student who wanted to push their luck. One colleague mentioned his intelligence, while another described how Peter was

> 'fragile, formal yet friendly, precise but not pedantic' . . . he would spot pupils' potential and gently push them to fulfil it. Despite his old fogey image, he had an acute understanding of the problems of modern adolescent boys. For some he became almost like a second father.
>
> Peter resisted the progressive elements in English teaching during the 1970s, and had hoped to become a headmaster.

All the same essential tropes are there, and it would be relatively easy to substitute 'Alexander Scott' for Peter Farquhar. Even the fact that it is Michael Crick who is writing the obituary is an echo of the fictional Scott's former pupils, who go on to become 'serious journalists working for broadsheet newspapers'.

Perhaps what is most interesting is that the characters of Alexander Scott and the Reverend John Donaldson are both needed to accommodate the personal issues and dilemmas that Peter wanted to discuss. One character clearly wasn't enough to communicate everything that he wanted to say, although this wasn't just about the breadth of what it was that he wanted to examine. Instead this 'splitting' allows him to compartmentalise and separate not only his faith from his sexuality, but also his love of literature and how the teaching of it was changing in ways that he disliked.

As should be made clear, I am also deliberately employing here the Freudian idea of splitting. I am hinting at something wider and more personal to Peter. Splitting in this more psychoanalytic sense is a defence mechanism for the ego when faced with conflicting interpretations, or representations, of the self. It allows that individual to find a way to accommodate both his instinctual demands and the need for these passions to be gratified, by recognising their incompatibility with reality. Do sensual pleasures and altruism have to be incompatible? Splitting is therefore not about denying reality, but finding ever more creative ways to avoid it.

*

I would have liked to have built up a deeper picture of Peter at Stowe, given how important teaching was in his life, but many of the teachers I approached didn't really want to speak to me. They were of course far too polite to deny me outright, and those who did agree wanted to speak off the record. In the end, I conducted five such interviews, although their contents would hardly be illuminating for the reader as I would have to hide too many details. I was intrigued both by my interviewees' reticence, or their desire for anonymity, especially as everyone I spoke to, including those who refused to be interviewed, were adamant about one thing: they absolutely hated *Between Boy and Man*.

Their intense dislike of the book ranged from its homoerotic subplot, which was seen as perpetuating a myth about boarding schools (or was this simply old-fashioned homophobia in another guise?), to the fact that they saw the novel as damaging the 'brand' of Stowe, given that Moreton College was very clearly about the school and people who had taught, or still worked, there. One interviewee was particularly aggrieved by what they presumed was their own portrayal in the book, and one or two others gleefully pointed out which character equated to an actual member of staff in real life.

Another said, rather confusingly, that they wouldn't speak to me as they 'didn't want to get involved'. I was baffled. In what way, I wondered, did they feel that by talking to me they would become 'involved' in a case where the victim had been killed, his murderer arrested, charged, tried, convicted and sent to prison?

I was particularly interested by the observation that the book had damaged the school's 'brand' or, as it was put to me, 'wasn't helpful'. What did these statements mean? I tried to be sensitive and understand in what way it was not helpful, and how it had damaged the school's brand, although frankly I was confused. It was a work of fiction, after all, and *Between Boy and Man* was almost gushing in its delight at the intelligence of the children who went there. Exactly what part of the brand was being damaged? Several Old Stoics, as former pupils are known, of my acquaintance always joked that the school was best known for recruiting 'the cream of the country – rich and thick'. That's clearly not true, but that was the informal way the school was thought of – so much so that the Channel 4 comedy drama *Fresh Meat*, set in a fictional university, deliberately used a posh, dim character called Jonathan Pembersley, 'JP' (played by Jack Whitehall), who inevitably went to Stowe, in exactly that way.

This was all very interesting, but the teachers' silence, or desire for anonymity, left me with a problem. I needed to find a way to make Stowe come to life.

*

First, I tried their advertising.

The school's clearly cutting edge, and no doubt costly, website describes Stowe as 'an extraordinary school set within a beautiful ducal palace and historic landscaped gardens'. All of this is true, of course, but both the ducal palace and the landscaped gardens predate the school by several centuries.

One of the most famous Old Stoics was the English actor David Niven. In his best-selling autobiography, *The Moon's a Balloon,* he describes how the school was founded in 1923, not 'by Kings, Archbishops or Lord Mayors but by a consortium of educators and hard-headed businessmen who saw the possibilities for a new public school and hoped to make a good thing out of it'. Niven loved the school, and was particularly taken by the first headmaster, the Edinburgh-born John Fergusson Roxburgh. J. F. Roxburgh made certain that he taught every pupil at some stage of their time at the school; he loved passing on to them his own love of literature.

Another famous Old Stoic is the entrepreneur Sir Richard Branson, who did not have such a happy time at school. Dyslexic and not very good at sports, Branson left at sixteen and has said, 'I can't say I enjoyed it enormously.' He would subsequently send his own children to school in Oxford. Bob Drayson, the headmaster at the time, apparently said to the departing Branson, 'Congratulations, Branson. I predict you will either go to prison or become a millionaire.'

Back on Stowe's website, the current headmaster, Dr Anthony Wallersteiner, who joined the school in 2003, the year before Peter retired, assures prospective parents that 'Stowe embodies the English Enlightenment and the values and ethos of this epoch continue to shape the people who teach and learn here.' Well, let's leave to one side what the headmaster means when he talks of 'the English Enlightenment', and instead interrogate what these values and the ethos might be. He says that 'each boy and girl is treated as an individual', and that a 'Christian ethos encourages pupils to develop a lasting sense of moral, social and spiritual responsibility'.

Elsewhere on the school's website, we are told how 'our Day Pupils play a full part in school life' and contribute to Stowe's 'vibrant, friendly and inclusive community'. As such, two 'bespoke Day Houses' have been opened. The fees for day pupils are just over £20,000 per annum, which is roughly half of what it would cost to board.

This is all part of responding to 'the challenging market'. In other words, English middle-class families – especially if they have more than one child – simply cannot afford fees of nearly £40,000 per annum, and therefore different markets had to be opened up. Making a profit is surely one of the core values of the school too.

Day pupils were one market, but there were others, and one of those got Stowe into difficulties. In 2016, David Fletcher, Stowe's then registrar, accepted an invitation to go to Claridge's in London by a representative acting on behalf of a Russian businessman, who was seeking a place at the school for his son. In reality, and obviously unbeknown to Fletcher, this representative was actually an undercover reporter for the *Telegraph*. There was no Russian businessman.

Over a glass of wine, Fletcher was secretly recorded explaining that what he was going to say was 'going to start sounding a bit dodgy', but 'I always say to my headmaster ... you just don't realise how things operate elsewhere, and also you just don't understand that some of these people are rich beyond Croesus.' The registrar said that he received calls all the time from rich foreign families or, as they were described, 'the global super-rich', and that 'there is now this kind of code' that they were 'keen to work with Stowe'. In other words, in return for a donation of £100,000, 'or something like that', a child of borderline academic ability would be allowed in. Fletcher was unambiguous that this was now a 'growth industry', as 'private education prices itself out of the market with British families, many schools are having to go down that international route just to stay afloat'.

When this journalistic sting was revealed to the school, Fletcher resigned. After all, bribery and corruption hardly sit well with the values and ethos of the 'English Enlightenment', or indeed with the law of the land.

Dr Wallersteiner denied any knowledge or involvement with what Fletcher had done, but he has not escaped controversy himself during his tenure as headmaster. In May 2019, he told *The Times* that 'the rise of populists and polemicists has created a micro-industry in bashing private schools', and likened the treatment of people educated privately to the Nazis' persecution of the Jews. He was particularly angered that the numbers of pupils from independent schools being accepted by Oxford and Cambridge was falling, and that more children from state schools were being accepted, describing this as a form of 'social engineering'. His comments caused a furore, with the editor of the *Jewish Chronicle* commenting that 'clearly the headmaster of Stowe is not an idiot ... but he is doing his best to convince people that he is', and Labour's Lord Adonis said: 'If the headmaster of Stowe believes his students are treated by university admission in the way Hitler treated the Jews, why does he think their parents pay £39,000 a year for the privilege?'

I have offered these vignettes not to poke fun at the school, but rather to indicate the emerging institutional culture that was antithetical to what Peter valued as a teacher and which he would later reflect in his own writing. Of course, quite apart from what is formally acknowledged there are often unspoken rules which shape an institution's culture, and which can have an impact on how an individual within that institution thinks, behaves and communicates. That culture can be welcoming and encourage a sense of belonging within that institution, but it can also make someone feel uncomfortable and excluded. My off-the-record interviews confirmed this analysis about the changing culture of Stowe and one or two of these interviewees suggested that it was one of the reasons that Peter had decided to take early retirement.

I was able to glean quite a bit from the school's website, but I also read through all of the back issues of *The Corinthian*, the magazine for Old Stoics. In the 2016 edition I came across a beautiful tribute to Peter by Crispin Robinson, one of his colleagues and a member of the Stowe Reading Group. It summed up what his life at Stowe had been like and his qualities as a teacher. Robinson said Peter was 'much revered', 'widely regarded as one of our best teachers', and continued:

At School he was a committed Christian, fully involved with the spiritual welfare of Stoics and staff. He prepared candidates for Confirmation and led Bible studies as well as often preaching in Chapel . . . Peter was firm in his deep and sincere Christian faith and may he rest in peace.

To allow me to continue to build a picture of Peter's life, I next turned to Professor Valerie Sanders. Valerie was a friend of Peter's, and a fellow member of the Stowe Reading Group.

*

Valerie would record in her diary that she hadn't really wanted to go.

Too late, too late.

She had accepted Peter's invitation and so, even if she wasn't in the mood, she didn't feel that she could now make her excuses and so she simply came to terms with the fact that she would indeed be attending her first meeting of the Stowe Reading Group. The SRG had been in existence for a couple of years before Valerie attended her first meeting, on 21 April 1993, and had an established order to its proceedings. It met three times a year, in January, April and September, at a different member's house each time. The host would choose the book to be discussed, and provide a two-course meal. Wine would be served. The meeting would start at 7 p.m. and continue until the discussion had ended, generally around 10 p.m., but sometimes much later than that. There were usually eight or nine formal members of the SRG at any one time; occasional guests might also be invited, or who asked to attend because they were interested in the book to be discussed.

Valerie had a sneaky suspicion that she had only been invited to become a formal member because they were short of women.

No one was in any doubt that Peter was in charge. Before the host was offered twenty minutes to outline the book they had chosen, Peter would conduct group business: who was next to choose a book and act as host; what date was best for everyone. It was, Valerie noted in her diary, 'formal and taken very seriously and not at all like other book clubs I've been a member of'.

This was, of course, the official culture of the SRG but, over time, Valerie learned that there were informal rules too – much like Middle England perhaps more generally. During one of our several telephone calls – coronavirus having put paid to meeting up in person – Valerie remembered that the SRG was quite 'blokeish' and there was 'this courtliness to proceedings. The women attending were at all times served food first; I remember too being offered the best chair to sit on. Nice in their own way, but it served to remind me that I – my gender – was in a minority.' It also had a 'soft, Christian and Anglican undertone that cut all the way through. I was always being advised that I should take up bell-ringing, which wasn't really the sort of thing a Jewish girl would ever actually do.'

Above all else, it was an unwritten rule that the books had to be 'serious – no Jilly Cooper was allowed; nothing like that, or anything that was seen to be too frivolous. It was a bit like Harriett Gilbert's series "A Good Read" on Radio 4.'

I first got to know Valerie after I moved to Buckingham, through a mutual acquaintance, my old history tutor Professor Bruce Collins, who was now teaching at UB. We met socially many times and so I got to know her well and, inevitably, I remember her talking about the SRG. I know that Valerie didn't really mind the seriousness of the SRG, even if, looking back, she admits that she seems to have recorded in her diary just as much about where the meetings were held, the decor of the rooms, the furnishings and especially the quality of the food that was served, as she had about their discussion of the books. 'Serious' came as second nature to Valerie, although that inadvertently served to mask her warm sense of humour.

She'd been born in Hull and had read English at Cambridge, before completing her DPhil at Oxford in 1982. Her doctoral dissertation had been about the prolific Victorian writer, intellectual and sociologist Harriet Martineau. On the day that she left Oxford, Valerie had been given her first academic post at the University of Buckingham and was to stay there for almost fifteen years, before taking up academic appointments at Sunderland and then finally returning home in 2001, by becoming Professor of English at the University of Hull.

When I asked her why she had accepted Peter's invitation at all, she thought about it carefully and then said:

It was an event; a big deal; it was about books – and of course I taught literature at the local university. I thought that it would also allow me to develop my social life in Buckingham, but outside of the university. [Pause] I suppose I was also a bit intrigued; I was curious about how other people lived. I'm a northern urbanite; a woman with a Jewish heritage and, well, they were southern, Anglican and had lived in this small country market town for most of their lives. They were different. I know that I have made this all sound very serious, but there was a lot of laughter too, and I did rather like getting an occasional meal in a rambling country house.

The SRG might only have met three times a year, but the people who attended clearly became a circle of friends. They

offered support and companionship outside the formal meetings of the book club.

In fact, Valerie enjoyed the SRG so much that she would
continue attending meetings after leaving Buckingham, and
remained a member until 2008. She can therefore become
our host at these meetings too, which will help us to build up
a picture of the books that Peter liked, disliked, and how he
would go about making an argument. We can catch a glimpse
of this literary Peter, not just through his novels, but from a
friend who sometimes stayed in his house, and got to know
how he thought, behaved and acted in company.

The week after her first meeting, perhaps as some form
of reward for increasing the number of women, Peter asked
Valerie to an event at Stowe School. Peter had invited Dame
Iris Murdoch and her husband Professor John Bayley to host a
joint discussion about 'The English Novel Today', after which
dinner would be served. Peter suggested that Valerie should
read Murdoch's *The Message to the Planet* and *Nuns and
Soldiers* before coming, and she would sit next to Bayley at
dinner. She remembered that Murdoch and Bayley had 'been a
bit slow to get going, and I couldn't quite get this image of them
eating poached eggs on toast for breakfast out of my mind, but
once they warmed up it was pretty lively'. Their conclusion,
perhaps predictably, despite the fact that Murdoch was still
writing novels at this time, was that the English novel today
wasn't as good as it had been in the nineteenth century. The
event also made Valerie aware of how well connected Peter
was and just how far his acquaintances stretched. 'Looking
back,' she said, 'he had clearly come across, or known, some
very distinguished people.' She was also pleased that 'he felt

able to talk to me about literature and writing – his own, as well as other people's writing. I got to know him well, but on reflection I realise now that he was still quite a private person.'

Surely, I said to Valerie, there must have been some discussion about sexuality in a few of the books that were chosen by the SRG, which might have opened up more intimate areas of discussion. Valerie thought about this, and said she would look through her notes and diaries and then get back to me.

*

Peter was always well prepared for the meetings of the SRG and, like a good teacher, he had a particular way of contextualising the book under discussion. Valerie described his approach:

> Peter's was, I think, an orthodox approach. He'd outline the plot and pick out some themes which he thought were important and central. It was also an accessible way of getting into the book because you have to remember that there were some 'amateur readers' who also attended, and so you couldn't approach the novel too formally. He was particularly good at picking up on weaknesses in the plot, but he would also consider language, characterisation and what, ultimately, was 'the point of it all'. He wasn't teaching per se and so, for example, he wasn't thinking about what an examiner might want to see in a script, and was much more, like a lecturer would, skimming the surface over some things, but going into greater depth in other places. It was rigorous.

Valerie remembers staying at Peter's house after an SRG meeting in October 2006; the next morning Peter had discussed with her the plot of the novel that would become *Between Boy and Man*. Peter sat taking notes on the points that Valerie made, and she recorded in her diary that 'afterwards, he said awkwardly, he hoped I didn't think the situation discussed in the novel was his. I couldn't decide if this was a coded way of telling me he wasn't gay, but he seems to me a man who doesn't have any romantic interest in women.' She added that, to her, he seemed like a 'repressed/celibate gay man' but that 'evidently he didn't want me to think that *Between Boy and Man* was about him, but I would see him in that book as Alexander Scott and imaginatively projected onto the Rev D and what might happen if...'

Let's think about that 'if' that trails away in her diary entry.

Having looked through her notes, Valerie remembered that the book that Peter had most enjoyed and which he had himself proposed when he hosted the SRG in April 2006 had been Alan Hollinghurst's *The Line of Beauty*. This choice, coming as it did two years after he had retired from Stowe, seems very significant, especially as it has an openly gay narrator, Nick Guest. Nick is a charming, handsome English graduate from Oxford, who had lusted over the straight and unobtainable Toby Fedden, the son of Gerald Fedden, a Tory MP, while they were at university together. After graduating, he rents a room in the attic of the Feddens' home in London. Nick is therefore a 'guest' by name, and by his domestic arrangements. Nick's sexuality is never revealed to the Feddens. The action is set in the 1980s, not only at the height of Thatcherism but also when the consequences of HIV and AIDS were beginning to change gay subculture.

Nick was supposedly in London to write his PhD on Henry

James and, according to a review in the *New Yorker,* 'like a Jamesian hero, he subsumes deeper longings into an aestheticized fixation with handsome lovers and with the Feddens' elegant world – a reverie that is shattered by public scandal and by AIDS'.

Valerie wrote in her diary that Peter 'talked too lengthily about *The Line of Beauty* which the others quite liked, but were less enthusiastic than I was'. She noted that Peter shared with the others how he wasn't certain 'if Nick was a genuine observer, or a self-seeking social sponger'; that he was like Pip in *Great Expectations;* that the novel was filled with a constant threat of disapproval; that there were consequences if you took risks with sex and drugs; and of the divided personality of Nick himself. Finally, Valerie added that Peter had discussed how 'Nick had started to talk just like the Feddens, so that, by the end of the novel, he had begun to sound like them'.

The parallels between Nick Guest and Ben Field are obvious. To take the most immediate examples: Field, just like Nick, started out as a guest in another person's house although, as his own emails would reveal unambiguously, he really was simply a self-seeking sponger; and both were undertaking PhDs in English literature. However, what is perhaps of greater interest is that Peter's choice of this book – the first time, as far as Valerie can remember, that a novel with a gay theme had been chosen at the SRG – reveals, in her words, how 'this period of post retirement, but pre-Ben Field was a creative but perhaps also a turbulent time for [Peter] when he was confronting some tough issues about himself and his emotional and sexual needs'.

Valerie's final attendance at the SRG was on 12 April 2008

and, ironically, the title of the book they had discussed that night was *The Reader*, by Bernhard Schlink. By then comfortably settled in Hull, Valerie just couldn't face the four-hour train journeys, with at least one change, down to Buckingham and then back up to the north-east three times a year.

It was time to move on.

Sadly, Valerie was never to see Peter again.

CHAPTER THREE

A Meeting of Minds

'As if possessed by magic powers, the monster
had blinded me to his real intentions'

MARY SHELLEY,
Frankenstein

I n January 2010, nineteen-year-old Ben Field was part of
the new intake onto the University of Buckingham's BA
in English literature. The university, eager to encourage local
students, awarded him a Sir Ray Tindle scholarship worth
£1000. As well as his major in literature, Field also took a
minor in journalism. After speaking with Valerie I thought
that the next part of my research should be trying to understand more about Field and his time at the university. So, as
part of my research, I arranged to meet up with one of his
lecturers, the former *Birmingham Post* and *Daily Telegraph*
journalist Roger Perkins. Roger would prove to be one of my
most insightful interviewees – he takes forthright to a whole
new level of plain-speaking, and he told me that there would

be 'no smoke, no mirrors, and no interpretation' in what he said. He agreed to meet me in the Vinson Building café on campus, to help me to form an impression of what Field had been like as a student at UB.

I parked my car in Well Street, outside the Woolpack, and then slowly wandered down by the river, past the disused football stadium where Buckingham Town used to play, close to the tennis courts and then through some well-tended grassy expanse in the direction of the university. The sun was shining, the river gurgled pleasantly and the sound of birdsong accompanied me on my short walk. Ah, Middle England.

The University of Buckingham (UB) likes to brand itself as 'the home of the two-year degree' and 'the university where students come first'. At least one of these statements is true. It has just over two hundred staff, and its nearly 3500 students are spread over two main campuses, in London Road and Hunter Street. The London Road site – opposite the town's swimming pool – contains the Franciscan Buildings, where the law school is situated, but by far the most important part of the university is clustered around Hunter Street, the 'riverside campus'. There, in a south-turning bend of the Great Ouse's lazy flow through the town, the university has quietly established its most important buildings.

The beautiful Georgian Yeomanry House houses all of the university's administration; the Anthony de Rothschild Building is the home of economics and business; the university's library is also located on this site; and the Tanlaw Mill, on the opposite side of the road, is the home of a refectory and the Student Union. In November 2018, the university opened the Vinson Building on the riverside campus, and this now accommodates UB's largest lecture theatre, a bookshop and café, and has study spaces for students. I drafted a great deal of this book in the café before COVID-19 made its mark, scribbling away as students came and went, eagerly chatting about their loves and their lives. That's what students do; some occasionally also study.

To the east of Hunter Street are Station and Chandos Roads, and, overlooking the river, the Chandos Building. The Chandos Building also has a large lecture theatre and associated classrooms and staff offices, and plays an important role in this story, as it is where students enrolled on UB's degree in English literature are taught.

I hadn't met Roger Perkins before, but I recognised his picture from some advertising on the university's website, and so when he came into the café I gave him a cheery wave. We found ourselves some seats and pretty soon, over flat whites, we were discussing quite openly his impressions of Field and the case more generally. Roger, a historian by training and now in his early sixties, was as plain-speaking as he had promised he would be.

He painted me a picture of Field's first few weeks at UB, and then offered a more general insight into his former student's personality. He remembered that Field 'started off quietly, but he came across as a bit snide – laughing at other people's contributions. I kept thinking, Be nice. Behave. Other students were struggling with the culture and the language [UB has a significant number of overseas students], but he'd just roll his eyes if they said something that he didn't think was up to scratch.'

Roger described Field as having 'clever-boy syndrome', and

that he was a 'humblebragger'. This was an oxymoronic term that I didn't understand, and so I asked Roger to explain:

> He said things to make it appear that he was humble, but it was actually about trumpeting his achievements. He said he could do sign language in an 'aren't I clever' way, although I never saw him use it, or anyone else say that they had seen him use it. Whether he could or not, it was a concealed boast to draw attention to himself. He wasn't as clever as he thought and his arrogance really shone through.

Roger drained his coffee and concluded the first of our meetings by observing, 'He might have been able to bamboozle his teachers when he was at school, but he didn't cut any ice with me.'

This insight into Field's personality as a student corresponded with what I had learned from my initial research about him during his time at school, and which Roger was alluding to at the end of our discussion. Field was the middle child of Ian and Beverley Field, and had been raised in Market Harborough in Leicestershire, where his mother had been a Liberal Democrat councillor between 2003 and 2009. The family had moved to Olney in Northamptonshire in 2008, where Ian had become the minister at Olney Baptist Church. The Fields were described as 'the backbone of the community' in Olney, and it is clear that they brought up their three children – Ben, his older sister Hannah and his younger brother Tom – to value education and to have a good work ethic. As for his schooling, Field attended the Bishop Stopforth School in Kettering, where he obtained three A levels: an A in English literature, an A in music and a C in economics. These were good results, but they were not outstanding, and the C in economics must have been especially galling, as Field liked to think of himself as an intellectual cut above his peers.

Years later, as his former classmates lined up to offer snap-shots of Field's schooldays, they'd present an inconsistent portrait of what he had been like. Some thought that he had been aloof, while others described him as having been popu-lar. One remembered that he had run a campaign to become head boy – but he didn't succeed. However, one thing that they all agreed on was that Field liked to be thought of as 'super-intelligent', and that he 'was in love with his own intellect'. He also claimed to have written a romantic novel for Mills & Boon, although this has never been proven. One old school friend remembered that Field would skip classes so that he could go to the library, where he'd memorise words from the dictionary. Armed with this knowledge he'd try to catch out his teachers, and was sometimes accused of patronising them if he believed that he knew more about a subject than they did.

Patronising, of course, means to appear kind and helpful, but that appearance betrays a feeling of superiority or conde-scension. What you see is not what you get.

Perhaps it is significant that Field would go on to target a teacher, and then set out to bewitch at least one lecturer that he encountered.

*

The university and the literature that was taught there is cen-tral to understanding the origins and nature of this murder, and can provide new insights into both the perpetrator and his victim. However, as more salacious and sensational details emerged, reporting about the case became dominated by the infatuations and motivations of individuals – especially in relation to their sex lives. The importance of the institutions which nurtured and shaped the behaviour of these individuals, or provided the context in which the events of the murder would unfold has therefore remained obscured.

For me, it is impossible to truly make sense of what happened to Peter without an appreciation and understanding of this institutional, academic and literary context. To use a more criminological analysis, in this case they are the 'nurture' mechanisms of that staple question about offenders: is it in their nature to commit crime, or a consequence of how they have been nurtured?

A little history is helpful at this point.

The University of Buckingham traces its origins to a letter published in *The Times* on 27 May 1967. The letter was written by a somewhat obscure physician, Dr J. W. Paulley, who had spent time in America. In his letter he argued that it was now right to create 'at least one new university in this country on the pattern of those great private foundations in the USA, without whose stimulus and freedom of action the many state institutions in that country would be much poorer'.

Paulley's vision was to create in the UK an American liberal arts college like Williams or Amherst in Massachusetts, or Swarthmore in Pennsylvania. In other words, a private university that was not dependent on government funding, but instead relied on the fees of its students and the generosity of its benefactors. This was controversial stuff, especially given the left-leaning post-war consensus that dominated the politics of the 1960s and 1970s, as it implied that state funding and subsidy was not the only – or even the best – economic model to deliver a university education.

That controversy was further stoked when the idea contained in Dr Paulley's letter became a reality and the University College of Buckingham was founded in 1973, when Margaret Thatcher was Secretary of State for Education, and received its first students three years later. As if to provide fuel to the ideological fire, the opening ceremony was performed by Mrs Thatcher, who by that time was leader of the Conservative Party and Her Majesty's Opposition. However, many people remembered her best from her tenure as Secretary of State for Education, when she infamously stopped the provision of free milk to primary school children – for which she earned the nickname 'Thatcher the Milk Snatcher'. In February 1983, with Mrs Thatcher now firmly embedded as prime minister, the University of Buckingham was incorporated by grant of Royal Charter. UB was clearly important to Mrs Thatcher – and to Thatcherism – and, on her retirement from politics, she served as the university's chancellor from 1992 to 1998.

There remains a lively debate about what 'Thatcherism' actually consisted of, but perhaps the key words that it became associated with – the touchstones of its philosophy – are illustrative. These words seemed to seep into public consciousness: freedom, self-reliance, individual choice, enterprise. All were allied to an authoritarian conservatism that emphasised morality and personal responsibility. These key words often became a shorthand for an oppositional view of the world, which characterised the politics of the 1960s and 1970s as 'socialist', and which in turn had created a 'culture of dependency'. Thatcherism was most certainly not about socialism or dependency, which meant that, as far as the economy was concerned, it opposed central planning and state control, whether of the mines, the steel industry, railways, public utilities, or even education.

UB therefore was, and to a certain extent has remained, an institution that fits rather neatly into a neoliberal view of the world, where there is no such thing as society and so every man, woman and child are mere atomised individuals striving only for themselves.

The original model might have been American liberal arts colleges like, for example, Williams or Swarthmore, but getting things up and running proved more problematic. In its early years, UB failed to attract many students, and those it did came almost entirely from overseas. In a 2003 article published in the *Guardian* about how Labour might be able to deliver on its target of 50 per cent of under-thirties entering higher education by 2010, Will Woodward, the paper's education editor, visited UB. As part of his visit he interviewed Terence Kealey, at the time UB's vice-chancellor, who honestly reflected that the university's existence was akin to being 'a pioneer, *pour encourager les autres* ... Buckingham is really about changing Oxford, Cambridge, Imperial and Warwick, saying to them, "come on in, the water's lovely".' UB was therefore not only a bit of an experiment, but also a potential model for the delivery of higher education to ever greater numbers of students – the 'water' that was 'lovely' was self-sufficiency, rather than government grants and subsidies. So surviving as an institution meant attracting greater numbers of students and developing a much more commercial understanding of what universities taught, and how that offering was structured.

As Kealey saw it, 'We have a customer called the student, and we are obsessed with the customer. Everything is there to cater for the student.' The downside to this focus was, as Kealey admitted, 'scholarship is something that is not prized as much'. As for the liberal arts vision? Kealey accepted that UB 'was not created to be what it has become. It has become a vocational school for law and business for non-British students, because that's where the market has taken us.'

The market. I was reminded of the 'challenging market' facing Stowe School, which had set off a series of changes that had led to Peter taking early retirement. And what was true of Stowe was equally important within HE. The 'market' continues to be a dirty word within HE; a crude mechanism to turn education into a commodity, like soap powder, toilet paper, or cars. Pile it high and sell it cheap. And, of course, this commercialisation could take universities into areas that might make them money, but not necessarily contribute to understanding, scholarship, knowledge, or the greater good of the individual, or indeed of society as a whole – if you believed that such a thing actually existed. As Kealey was honest enough to admit, a university with a commercial ethos follows the cash. The liberal arts college had become a vocational school, much in the same way as Stowe had attempted to attract the 'global super-rich' and open new day houses to keep the home-grown children of the middle class coming.

A great many of UB's students were and continue to come from Asia or Africa, and they are particularly attracted to the university's full-time two-year degree. Students study for forty-eight weeks of the year and do not have the long summer holidays that stretch an undergraduate degree at other universities into three years, so they really can get their degree at UB in two years – just like it says on the tin.

Terence Kealey made one other point that is worth noting. He said that UB 'blends quietly into its small town'. Students don't really get noticed in Buckingham – not just because there are relatively few of them but also those who do come from overseas don't need part-time jobs in the town to supplement their income. Nor do they socialise in Buckingham. The attractions of a small, ancient, overwhelmingly white market town can't really compete with what's on offer half an hour's drive away in Oxford, or further afield in multi-cultural London. Perhaps the only locals who regularly encounter the students are the town's taxi drivers. Over the years I have lost count of the stories I have been told of student fares being picked up at their halls of residence and then dropped off less than a mile away in Hunter Street for their lectures. Seemingly, they tip very generously.

However, when I started to poke beneath the surface a little more deeply, I discovered that there were local resentments about students and the university more generally which, as far as some residents were concerned, had merely served to inflate rents in the town.

As Kealey suggested, buildings can hide students and their lecturers, but people, in turn, can hide themselves – even if they are all too visible in the community. Some can dazzle with the force of their personality, while all the time hiding their true characters and intentions. That character is not created overnight, but built over time, shaped by family, friends and institutions. It is my job as a criminologist to reconstruct that character and show how it was first created, and then shaped and moulded. That's how I begin to make sense of the senseless and how I try to understand what might have driven someone to take the life of another human being.

In the past two decades many other universities have embraced the market. UB is certainly not the only university with a marketing budget that it uses to advertise itself with some care, so as to better sell its academic wares. However, as the leader of the trend, UB is perhaps more astute and so has continued to grow, and has recently added a medical degree to its 'offering'. Another measure of its growing appeal is the number of students it now attracts from England and Wales. This domestic recruitment has been aided by the fact that student loans can now be obtained to study at UB, and a potential student might quickly calculate that a two-year degree is much cheaper to fund than one that takes twelve months longer.

Benjamin Field was one of these calculating students.

*

Given the way that his degree was structured, Field did not encounter Peter as a lecturer until his second year, in April 2011. Peter taught a module on Romantic literature, which he coordinated with Dr Setara Pracha, who continues to teach at the university – and who we will talk more about later. This wasn't a module about books from within the canon of Mills & Boon; the subject matter wasn't about dashing doctors sweeping chaste nurses off their feet, or heroic pilots falling madly in love with air stewardesses, all the time skilfully landing a plane on one engine with no fuel left in the tank.

It wasn't romantic in that way; the capital R is important.

At the very least, the capitalisation suggests that this was a key evolutionary moment in Western literature. In one sense, Romantic literature, or Romanticism, is simply a convenient label for literature produced between 1789 and 1832. Both dates are significant. The first is of course the start of the French Revolution, and the latter is when Sir Walter Scott died (who, along with Robert Burns, was one of the most important Scottish Romantics) and when the Great Reform Bill passed into law. Romanticism was radical and ideological – it wanted to change the world – and used the language of ordinary people, as opposed to the 'King's English', to do so. It was interested in everyday life; in joy, horror, awe and melancholy. It was especially interested in the power of nature, rather than science and the scientific thinking of the Enlightenment, which had powered the Industrial Revolution, and those broader social and economic changes that we have come to call modernity.

The module involved reading Jane Austen (who isn't really a Romantic at all, but was simply writing during this period), Samuel Taylor Coleridge, John Keats, Percy Bysshe and Mary Shelley and William Wordsworth. Wordsworth stands out here, for, as Professor Jonathan Bate recently put it, he always 'lacked the glamour of Coleridge' and 'failed to make the romantic career move of dying young or going mad'.

Peter was well acquainted with these authors, as they are the fundamental building blocks of A-level English literature, although his own literary tastes were wide and varied. We know something of these from the Stowe Reading Group. Quite apart from the Romantics, Peter enjoyed authors such as Henry James and Graham Greene, and more contemporary authors including Iris Murdoch, with whom, as we have seen, he was on friendly terms, Ian McEwan and A. S. Byatt.

After having retired from Stowe, partly to fulfil his own writing ambitions, Peter had taken up a part-time teaching post at UB and had brought something of the classroom into the lecture theatre. After his death, his former students were quick to praise Peter's teaching style and, above all, how he could make his subject matter exciting and lively. Given his previous association with Stowe, it was relatively easy to bring Romanticism to life, by using the school's buildings and its superb landscaped gardens, which are dotted about here and there with follies, to illustrate those staples of Romantic litera-ture: the power of nature, the sublime and the gothic. So, Peter organised a trip to the school for his students and afterwards invited them all back to his house for lunch.

This visit and the following lunch were to set in motion a series of events that would ultimately lead to Peter's death.

*

We know a great deal about this visit and what the lunch was like, as Field noted down what had happened in an email – which would, much later, become important evidence. After his arrest, the police found and then subsequently released to the press a great deal of Field's emails, notes, poems, cards, chat logs – where he went by the name 'StAbleMan' – and other miscellaneous writings, although it is sometimes dif-ficult to determine who Field was writing to, or why he had chosen to keep this material. As for this first lunch, we know that he attended with his friends Callum and Max, plus 'two boring students and an octogenarian Nigerian', and a young man called Miles. No mention is made of Martyn Smith, another student at UB and a part-time magician, with whom Field would go on to establish a business and who would eventually be charged along with Field, but acquitted. Miles was somewhat jealously described by Field as 'young faced and of Etonian stock' and 'the type of young man Peter feels great attraction for. By this he means "masturbates over".' In this same email, Field would moralistically describe Peter as a 'closeted, Christian, homosexual English teaching pedant with a serious problematic attraction to teens, and who continues to privately tutor fourteen- and fifteen-year-old boys in his house'.

As for the lunch itself, Field thought it 'a somewhat dragging affair. Pleasant enough and [Peter] invited any and all of us to return.'

Peter, on the other hand, found Field to be a 'delightful young man' and 'an absolute delight'. No doubt they would have spoken about their love of literature in this first meeting, which must have done much to make Field seem attractive and personable from the outset. After all, 'delightful' means charming, wonderful, enchanting and agreeable.

Field would take Peter up on his offer to return to his house in Maids Moreton, but not before he had tried to impress Peter during his lectures. He was trying to catch his eye; he wanted to stand out, as much as he wanted to fit in. Field described how he was 'his usual competitive self' with his peers, and that Peter 'valued my contributions'. We have only his word for that, although it is clear that at one stage Peter did think of his student as a 'serious intellectual'. However, it is worth noting that, for Field, being 'impressive' was always about putting someone else down.

For him to succeed, someone else had to fail.

*

Let's consider for a moment one of the books that Peter would have taught to Field as part of the Romantic literature module: Mary Shelley's *Frankenstein*. I knew the monster in the novel from film adaptations – perhaps the best-known monster in the history of motion pictures – and wondered if the book offered any clues as to Field and Peter's developing relationship. My research would prove fruitful.

Like no other novel that I know, *Frankenstein* seems to me to be a book which has been destroyed by its popularity. Long before I came to actually read it as part of my research, I wrongly believed that I understood the story, the characters and the plot. I considered it to be a simple gothic horror story that I was already familiar with, through watching James Whale's 1931 adaptation starring Boris Karloff as the monster and, perhaps more scandalously, Mel Brooks's 1974 comedy *Young Frankenstein*.

Despite emanating from two very different eras and genres, both films play on similar ideas related to the monster as innocent and childlike; its creator as either deluded or mad, but certainly god-like; and the existence of minor characters who helped Doctor Frankenstein in his experiments – a hunchback called Fritz in the 1931 movie, and Igor (superbly played by Marty Feldman) in *Young Frankenstein*.

I took the novel on a trip to New Zealand and, on the plane there and back and in between hiking, biking and boating (and a memorable sheep-shearing exhibition), I read it for the very first time.

Reading the novel was to open up its subtleties, and its great intellectual ambition. The book has a number of layers, and several themes sustain the narrative, including human rights, personal responsibility and, above all, the status of the body of knowledge that we call science and the dangers of applying or extending that knowledge without thought or caution. In one sense, *Frankenstein* is a science-fiction novel rather than a gothic horror story: a dystopian warning about the limits of scientific knowledge, and how that knowledge might be applied.

Sadly, I was to discover that there was no hunchback assistant.

Mary Shelley began writing the novel when she was eighteen, and the first edition was published anonymously in 1818, when she was twenty years old. Her name did not appear on the book until the second edition was published in 1821. As is well known, it began life as a competition between Mary, her new and rather dissolute husband Percy, who had abandoned his wife to elope with Mary, and Lord Byron, to see who could write the best horror story. Mary won.

The novel, almost as much as Frankenstein's monster himself, is stitched together using three different people: three different narrators to tell the tale of the monster and its creator. These voices are Victor Frankenstein; a sea captain called Robert Walton, who writes letters to his sister in England from his ship, describing his encounters with Frankenstein; and, finally, the monster that Frankenstein has created. The monster is variously called 'wretch', 'creature', 'fiend' and an 'abortion', and described as 'hideously deformed' and 'loath-some'. The story is told in flashback and Frankenstein, who is at the beginning of the novel following the monster to the North Pole in an effort to destroy it, encounters Walton on his increasingly frantic journey.

Of the inter-related themes of the novel, those which have the greatest relevance to what will eventually happen between Field and Peter concern the dangers of ambition and aspira-tion; the relation between Man and God, or the creator and the created; loss; silence; and solitude.

This last theme is apparent throughout the book. In one of the first letters that Walton writes to his sister, he says that 'I desire the company of a man who could sympathise with me . . . I have no one near me, gentle yet courageous, possessed of a cultivated as well as of a capacious mind, whose tastes are like my own, to approve or amend my plans.' Walton later writes that Frankenstein – who he had rescued on his jour-ney north – was the man he was looking for, 'the brother of my heart'.

Being alone was, for Walton, something to be regretted and therefore, if the occasion presented itself, rectified. He wanted a friend with whom he could share his thoughts and plans, and who had tastes similar to his own. He wanted a sympa-thetic male companion to share his life because he believed that would make his existence much richer and fuller. I don't think that it's pushing the analysis too far to suggest that Peter would have seen himself as Walton, and felt that he had found his 'gentle yet courageous' companion in Field.

And then there is silence.

Victor Frankenstein's narrative drives the more overtly

Romantic themes of the novel, especially in relation to dangerous knowledge. Frankenstein's descriptions of the various murders the monster has committed, or deaths the monster has been indirectly involved with, introduce the theme of silence which permeates the novel. At various points, Frankenstein could have acknowledged what he had done and then admitted to those in authority who he had created. He chooses not to do so, and that silence is to have profound consequences. More generally it is tempting to conclude it was this silence which created the context that allowed the monster to continue to get away with murder.

Frankenstein views the monster through the lens of the crimes that he has committed, but the monster sees things very differently. The monster wants to remind Frankenstein who created him. 'Remember that I am thy creature. I ought to be thy Adam, but I am rather the fallen angel, whom thou drivest from joy for no misdeed.' What is God's responsibility for and to his flock? What responsibility does a creator have for that which he has created? Clearly the monster would prefer to be Adam rather than the fallen angel but, above all else, he would like to have an identity. He would like to be human. The monster continually asks 'who am I?' and, in a telling passage, 'what was I? Of my creation and creator I was absolutely ignorant, but I knew that I possessed no money, no friends, no kind of property. I was, besides, endued with a figure hideously deformed and loathsome; I was not even of the same nature as man.'

One of the ways that the monster tried to overcome these disadvantages was to become a 'master of language', so that he could speak to the people he encountered – specifically a seemingly poor family who lived in a cottage that he secretly watched. He did not at first introduce himself to this family but simply observed their 'gentle manners and beauty' so that he could learn how to behave, as he wanted to be accepted by them; he wanted to fit in. We learn that the family had fallen on hard times, and that they were not really peasants at all. The monster hoped that if he embraced their culture it would create an identity for him which, in turn, would lead to his being admitted into their world. So he watched and listened; read; mirrored and mimicked. In this way he came to understand their habits, values and way of life, and became so fully in tune with them that 'when they were unhappy, I felt depressed; when they rejoiced, I sympathised in their joys'. However, he was ultimately rejected by the family and by others in the community, which merely added to his sense of injustice, isolation and loneliness – all of which he blamed on Frankenstein.

It doesn't seem too fanciful to suggest that these themes are repeated in Field's relationship with Peter, and in the subsequent murder. Of course Field was not 'hideously deformed' or 'loathsome' in his appearance; indeed, he would use his good looks as part of his seduction strategy. Field had that advantage over the monster. But the monster's lament, for example, that he possessed no money, no friends and had no kind of property could have been lifted straight from Field's writings and emails. Like the monster, Field – who had previously memorised words from the dictionary – mastered the language of those he wanted to seduce at the university, and more generally studied their habits and culture. He also boasted of having learned sign language. He wanted to be 'impressive' in class; to be the best and the brightest. In that respect, Field was very adept at giving the appearance of being what it was other people would like to see. To all the world he appeared to be a scholar and an academic; a student who cared about literature and the beauty of the written word; he wanted to show everyone that, in the words of Walton, he had a cultivated and capacious mind.

This is an aspect of the psychopathic personality: a tendency to mirror those who surround them, and to reflect back a manufactured and constructed image, as opposed to presenting a genuine and authentic picture of who they really are. The monster didn't convince the peasants, but Field clearly mesmerised and dazzled his academic peers and teachers.

We can perhaps also accept that, having lived all of his life as a single man, Peter might genuinely have wanted to have formed a relationship. To agree with this proposition is rather different from suggesting that Peter was lonely. After all, being in a relationship would provide a great deal of comfort and, while he did not create Field as Frankenstein had created his monster, Peter must have felt at the beginning of their relationship that he had found 'the brother of my heart'. Did he perhaps also feel that he had discovered and then nurtured a rare scholastic talent? Field would not have been the first student that Peter had taken under his wing. However, Peter was not to realise, perhaps until it was too late, that Field was an 'odious companion'.

*

At the end of the spring term in 2011 Field called Peter up and, as revealed in his writings, 'snake-talked' his way into his lecturer's house. In fact, Peter had already invited his students to visit him again, but it was only Field that took him up on that offer. As he described it:

> I called Peter and invited myself over. The reasons for this are manifold, but centre on avarice – I wanted to work at the university (where he was a guest lecturer), or at Stowe School (where he had been Head of English for 21 years), etc. So I went over and was amusing and cheered the poor man up. He retired early, to be a novelist, and his day-to-day existence was lonely.

As I have described, this idea that Peter was lonely would become a running theme in how the murder has been reported. It was also something that Field was keen to suggest as, ever the 'humblebragger', it served to paint him in a good light. However, there is also a world of difference between loneliness and being solitary and writers are often in the need of solitude, although this can sometimes be mistaken for being lonely. If Peter was serious about his writing – and he did go on to publish three novels – this would have involved extended periods of time with him being alone; being solitary. This does not fit easily with Freudian psychoanalytic theory, which takes as its starting point that humans are social beings who need companionship from the cradle to the grave, and that love is the only source of human happiness. Yet not all solitary people are without love or unhappy. We also need to recognise that Freud was wrong to suggest that our mental health is dependent on heterosexual fulfilment. We can have value as individual human beings whatever our sexuality, and not just as someone who fulfils a role as a spouse, or as a parent.

Field also recorded that after their relationship had become more established,

> I had, and still have, a very clear model of [our] relationship's reciprocity or mutuality, which is vulgarly commercial: he gives me things, and he gets me for a length of time. Historical example: he lets me stay in the spare room, makes me dinner and breakfast, and in exchange he wins at chess and feels a little less lonely.

This is yet another example of how Field likes to characterise Peter as lonely, but we also glimpse here something deeper, even if it remains self-serving. It's the 'vulgarly commercial' phrase that sticks out for me, as it seemed to indicate a basis for their relationship. However, I wondered to what extent that Field's 'vulgarly commercial' motivation transcended accommodation and meals. Above all we need to be careful about how we interpret these various editorials that Field very deliberately offers to us. I say deliberately, as we should remember that Field noted down his observations, filed them away and did not seek to destroy them. At the very least this suggests that he was not afraid of the light that they might show him in when they were eventually discovered. In other words, he is not ashamed of what he is describing: he's rather proud of being 'vulgarly commercial'.

A *quid pro quo* existed, is what Field wants us to believe. Peter only gets Field for 'a length of time', almost in the same way that a sex worker contracts with a client. This analogy has some basis in Field's reality, as it emerged in court that he used to sell sexual services. But, even though he would eventually sleep in the same bed as Peter, he also wants to infer something disreputable about his teaching of teenage boys, and adopts a rather disapproving moral tone, although, as far as I could uncover, there has never been any allegation of sexual misconduct against Peter, or that anyone else that I spoke to was aware of – including some of those teenage boys he had taught in his home.

It is also important to consider what else Field got out of his relationship with Peter. We should remember that this was a relationship initiated by Field, and clearly there was much more at stake than food and a bed for the night. Above all else, Field wanted access to Peter's contacts and saw using him as a means to further his own success, either at Stowe School or within the University of Buckingham. His relationship with Peter gave him credibility.

Peter was simply a means to an end.

And Field did succeed. He would graduate from UB with an upper second in January 2012. It was a good result but, in the same way that he must have been disappointed with his C in A-level economics, I get the distinct impression that he would have preferred a First. Seemingly, the problem was that he didn't do as well with his minor in journalism – perhaps because he couldn't 'snake-talk' and bluff Roger Perkins? However, his result was good enough to allow him to under-take an MA in English literature, which he completed in 2013. The university was so delighted by his dissertation on the contemporary Irish poet Paul Muldoon that the university press published it: *For 'Work' Read 'Work': Reading Ergodics and Ergodic Reading in Paul Muldoon* is still available on Amazon, where it has two five-star reviews – the first coming from Field's father Ian.

Not content with an MA, in January 2015, five years after first starting out on his undergraduate studies, Field enrolled on a PhD programme at the university. He really had become 'part of the furniture' and a 'poster boy for the university', as it was described to me: a familiar face on campus, a promising young scholar climbing the rungs of the academic career ladder.

By then he was living in Maids Moreton with Peter, and had started to work part time in the Red House Nursing Home.

*

This background that I have described must make us very careful when using Field's notes, emails, chat logs and diary entries. I believe that the notes that I have quoted, and Field's writing more generally, have a grooming quality to them – not just in what they reveal about how he went about grooming Peter, which is important to consider, but also in grooming us as readers. Field is snake-talking us too, and is doing so to control how this story is told. We can see this both in the idea that Peter 'wins at chess', which implies that he's being allowed to do so, and in the sense that we are expected to simply accept that Field was 'amusing' and therefore had brightened up Peter's otherwise lonely existence. I have no doubt that Field was charming in these initial encounters, but how reliable is he as a narrator of his relationship with Peter? We need to be careful about trusting his version of events, in the same way that we need to be wary of literary unreliable narrators such as Dr James Sheppard in Agatha Christie's *The Murder of Roger*

71

Ackroyd or Lou Ford in Jim Thompson's extraordinary *The Killer Inside Me.*

I am fascinated by Field's comment that his relationship with Peter developed for 'manifold' reasons. Was sex one of those many and varied reasons? There has been an assumption in the reporting of the case that it was Peter who was interested in the younger man, as opposed to the other way around, or that their relationship was asexual and simply platonic. A bed may have been shared and cuddles exchanged, but no more than that, we are led to believe. I wondered whose blushes were being spared – Field's, Peter's or even Middle England's? However, Field will not have been the first young man to become sexually interested in an older – sometimes much older – man, especially a man with wealth and influence. In his chat logs, written when he was still staying with Peter, he used the pseudonym 'StAbleMan' and those first two letters might suggest that he saw himself either as a 'saint', or as 'straight'. Perhaps he saw himself as both. Later in my research, I would discover that Field had sexual relations with an older woman, and so it is perhaps also worth considering whether Field was a gerontophile – someone who gains sexual pleasure from a much older partner.

Former classmates also offer very different perspectives of Field's sexual interests and about his sexuality. On the one hand he is described as a 'loner', and on the other as having had 'loads of girlfriends'. So too in the Radio 5 Live documentary presented by Jo Black, called *Killer in the Congregation*, which was broadcast after Field's conviction in 2019, it was revealed that Field would have covert sexual liaisons with men. Black's assertion was in all likelihood based on evidence from

Field's trial, where he admitted under oath to selling sexual services to men on at least five occasions. He'd 'received' oral sex, for which he was paid £30 to £50 on each occasion, he explained to the court. Again, we have only his word for the number of times that this might have occurred, but we can safely assume that he was trying to play things down on the witness stand, but his description merely poses the question: did he give as well as take in these encounters? Was he the lover, or the object of love? As a narcissist Field imagines that he is irresistible and therefore other people – everyone – must desire him, but at a psycho-dynamic level this merely served to confuse his own sexual orientation and interests. All in all I'm just as interested by the possibility that it was Field who desired Peter, despite the censorious tone that he had adopted about whom Peter tutored in his house and his exchanges on his chat logs, where it is suggested by one of his friends that it was Peter that 'want[ed] 2 bonk u just as bad'.

Taken together, it is possible to interpret Field's various writings as evidence of psychopathy, which I will discuss more fully in Chapter Eight. Here it is simply interesting to note that psychopathy is a personality disorder characterised by three features: an arrogant, glib and deceitful interpersonal style; risk-taking behaviour; and defective emotional responses.

Field is deceitful, hiding his true purpose for why he wants a relationship with Peter; he takes a risk in noting down his actions and thoughts and then keeping these notes, rather than destroying them (and has no insight into how they would be interpreted); and, finally, he seems incapable of truly understanding how Peter might feel. Peter merely exists for Field to use, and if this required making the relationship sexual then that, like for most psychopaths, would have been fine. Their relationship is, for Field, devoid of genuine feeling; it is only a means to an end. His 'vulgarly commercial' quip is so obviously glib and superficial that it initially takes the breath away, but it also hints at his underlying personality.

And, of course, when that relationship could no longer deliver what it was that Field wanted, or he had got from it all that he needed, it would be time to follow the market and move on to someone else.

Did Peter know this too? He was clearly a clever and educated man but, like Frankenstein in Mary Shelley's novel, perhaps 'the monster had blinded [him] to his real intentions' until it was too late.

*

If Field was indeed a 'monster' in this gothic, Romantic, literary sense, who should take responsibility for his creation? Peter did not create Field in the same way that Frankenstein created his monster. So who did? I have offered some insight into one of the institutions that nurtured Field but that can only get us so far in trying to answer one of the oldest and most fundamental questions in criminology and forensic psychology. I need to go further and answer the 'nature' half of the question too. All of this will take us into oppositional territory, which considers on the one hand the free will of an individual and, on the other, how that free will is constrained by forces beyond their personal control. These issues are important for, if we have free will, we can also be held responsible for our actions, but if we don't then blame has to lie elsewhere.

It is worth bearing in mind that the best answer to the 'nature vs nurture' question is almost always that it is a messy combination of the two: we are born, and we are made; it is in our nature and also how we have been brought up, and the relationships that we develop with our family, our friends and our peers. However, in thinking about how Field was 'nurtured' – especially in relation to his time at UB – we can easily see in him some of those values that characterise the university. I am not, of course, suggesting that UB condones murder. However, there is always a relationship between thinking and doing, being and becoming, and fantasy prompting action that is facilitated, or indeed constrained, by the specific place and circumstances that an individual inhabits. We are who we are by birth, but we are thereafter shaped and moulded by those institutions that we join, and the values and culture that surround us.

I am going to discuss more of Field's 'nature' later, but here I propose that, beyond Field's personal responsibilities for the crimes he committed, he was influenced by the institution where he studied, and which was founded on the values of individual action and freedom; private entrepreneurship rather than state funding; and a neoliberal world view that prioritised, in the words of the university's former vice-chancellor, following the market as a means to prosper. Field seems to have internalised those values completely and recognises this himself – he is 'vulgarly commercial'. He may have started out as someone who wanted to espouse liberal arts values, but he quite quickly descended into the murderous equivalent of a vocational school. In the criminological terms of ultra-realism, he was a criminal undertaker who granted himself the 'special liberty' to kill.

We can even interpret his notes and his emails as a form of

personal marketing and advertising. What he writes is therefore who he wants us to believe that he is, and he's proud of that person. He's most certainly not ashamed.

Let's end by again returning to *Frankenstein*.

As we have seen, two themes in the novel echo Peter's relationship with Field and the murder itself. These themes relate to silence, and finally to place. Frankenstein could have spoken out at several points in the narrative to reveal what he had created and who was responsible for the murders that had been committed. He did not. This silence is replicated in Field's relationship and subsequent murder of Peter. In Maids Moreton and in Buckingham – both the town and the university – no one publicly questioned, or challenged from a professional and ethical standpoint, what a student in his twenties was doing staying in the home of a man in his sixties, who was also at some stage responsible for that student's instruction and supervision at the university. No one intervened. Perhaps it was discussed in private, but in public people minded their own business and simply got on with their lives. Silence was the context in which Frankenstein's monster was able to kill, and also one which facilitated Field's deadly business. That context was so well established that if Field had stopped after having killed Peter, rather than targeting another elderly neighbour, he really would have got away with murder.

Place is an echo too and I get the impression that the town is still, even now, trying to come to terms with what happened. It was almost as if people imagined that it was impossible for a murder to take place in Buckingham and Maids Moreton as these could only occur in large, anonymous cities where people didn't know, let alone speak to their neighbours. Indeed, this was the most common recurring theme in conversations that I had with people living in Buckingham. Murder was something that people only read about in the newspaper, or saw on TV. It was not something that happened in Maids Moreton. As Trish on the Waitrose checkout put it to me: 'I can't believe it! Here! You'd never think that a murder could happen under our noses.'

But it did happen under our noses, and that reality woke people up to the fact that men – even those men who lived in Buckingham – could be 'monsters thirsting for each other's blood'. That gothic thought was both shocking and thrilling at the same time.

Of course, all murders take place within a specific space and setting, and in relation to Peter's death that place was Buckingham and its satellite village of Maids Moreton. And in the same way that the books Peter taught, those that he wrote and the culture of the university where he worked can reveal a great deal about his murder, so too does understanding a little more about Maids Moreton and Buckingham.

After all, as Frankenstein indicated, 'misery has come home'.

CHAPTER FOUR

Middle England

'if you can't adore yourself in the heart of the
nation, where can you?'

A. A. GILL,
Sunday Times, 2 May 2010

Buckingham has been my home for more than half my
life. I drink in its pubs, and eat in its restaurants; I
buy groceries at the local supermarket; my GP, dentist and
optician all work in the town; and, for almost as long as I
have lived in Buckingham, I've had an association with the
rugby club.

This background made me all the more conscious that
the communities of Maids Moreton and Buckingham were
curiously absent from both the Radio 5 Live and Channel 4
documentaries. As I have mentioned, the pictures used in the
latter, of a village green and a quaint church, were of a totally
different place – which felt to me downright lazy, and confused everyone in the town who watched the documentary.

That really won't do. Peter was murdered in plain sight in our community and so it is important to properly set the scene. And, given my long association with Buckingham, I feel comfortable about offering a little history, warts and all, by way of introduction to the town that likes to boast that it is the heart of England.

Until its noisy and rather bullying neighbour Aylesbury was gifted the title by Henry VIII, Buckingham was the county town of Buckinghamshire. Aylesbury is still the county town, but today Buckingham is much more likely to be bullied by the new kid on the block – Milton Keynes, whose creeping, crawling, seemingly unstoppable urbanisation threatens to one day swallow it whole. Aylesbury is now seen as a bit of an annoying joke, the sort of place that no one would ever want to admit that they had once lived or worked in, or had even just visited for the day. To be honest, Buckingham has always been very resilient to these new urban challenges and more besides for, over the centuries, it has had to deal with far worse and come to terms with warring Saxons, invading Danes and then all-conquering Normans.

The name Buckingham is derived from Old English, and means 'meadow of Bucca's people'. According to the ninth-century *Anglo-Saxon Chronicle*, the town was fortified by Edward the Elder in AD 918 to repel Danish invaders; Edward's stronghold is likely to have been on the site of the current parish church of St Peter and St Paul. In the Domesday Book, the town was recorded as belonging to Walter Giffard, who was made Duke of Buckingham by William the Conqueror. For much of the medieval era, Buckingham prospered as an important wool town, and a measure of that importance is that it had two market days and two annual charter fairs – which still take place today. There's still an open market in the town's square every Saturday. The Royal Latin School – also still in existence, although moved from its original site – was founded in 1423 by Edward VI.

As might be expected, Buckingham has had periods of prosperity and power, but also times of poverty and disaster, when it had little or no civic influence, often accompanied by dire financial circumstances. Gentry in the town, for example, had to decide if they were Royalists or Roundheads during the English Civil War, and tried to make a virtue out of not really choosing – even if privately the majority seemed to support the King. This approach didn't really work and the town might best be described as a 'frontier zone', where allegiances could change on an almost daily basis. In 1725, a fire wiped out most of the town's Georgian buildings (although Yeomanry House, now on the riverside campus of the University of Buckingham, escaped destruction) and Aylesbury capitalised on this misfortune by taking over the running of the assizes. The opening of what is now called the Old Gaol in 1748, the funding for its construction came mostly from Richard Temple, MP for the town and later Viscount Cobham, was an attempt to win the assizes back for Buckingham. It failed.

However, Buckingham has always bounced back from these civic and other failures and the history of the Old Gaol in many ways mirrors the history of the town. Over the years, after it stopped holding prisoners, the Old Gaol has served as a police station, a fire station, public toilets, a restaurant, an antiques shop and as a café; it is now a museum, and tries to attract visitors who enjoy 'dark tourism'. A grant from the

Heritage Lottery Fund in 2000 allowed for the addition of a glass roof over the original prisoners' exercise yard; I was delighted to perform the opening ceremony. The Old Gaol has been good at reinventing itself; of finding a way to make itself relevant to the present.

Perhaps more disastrous for the town's development than the fire of 1725 was the failure of Buckingham to be included on the line of the new London to Birmingham railway in the 1830s, partly due to opposition from the then Duke of Buckingham. As a result, the railway took a different course, through Wolverton, which has now been subsumed by Milton Keynes. It was only in 1850 that Buckingham became connected by rail, with its station constructed in Chandos Road. It didn't last for very long as the railway was closed in the 1960s, as part of the Beeching cuts. If you want to catch a train these days, you need to travel to Milton Keynes or, inevitably, Aylesbury.

Between 1841 and 1941, the town's population slowly decreased from four thousand to three thousand inhabitants. The steady and continuing growth in the numbers of people coming to live in the town is a trend that only started after the end of the Second World War. Ironically, many of the fifteen thousand people who now live in Buckingham would explain their decision to live in the town – as opposed to Milton Keynes or Aylesbury – as their having been attracted to its relative quiet. It is the absence of heavy industry, or the general hustle and bustle that might have come with more successful urbanisation, that has prompted Buckingham's growth. House prices are high, especially compared to other parts of Buckinghamshire, and residents don't seem to object to the lack of a rail link to get them further afield. However, by and large people do need a car to do their shopping at the various supermarkets that pepper the ring road, as only Waitrose and a small Tesco Express are located in the town centre. Like many towns, the market square has seen better days and charity and barber shops now seem to dominate, along with a surprising array of cafés. People say that they like the green space; the sense of history; the friendliness of the place; and, above all else, they usually hope their children might get into the grammar school.

When all is said and done, the market square notwithstanding, a crisis in Buckingham is much more likely to be an absence of sauvignon blanc in Waitrose than an increase in knife crime, muggings, or house burglaries. It is safe, predictable and, well, let's just admit it, sometimes a bit monotonous. Living in Buckingham can be like *Groundhog Day*. It really is the sort of place where everyone knows everyone else, although they'd also hate to think that they were prying or bothering you unduly. It's a town where new faces get noticed, although that seems to be changing, with more houses springing up on the ring road, and it is common for a stranger to offer you the unused portion of their ticket as you drive into town looking for a parking space. Sadly, that piece of casual civic altruism changed in late 2020, when the council introduced a new system that required you to enter your car registration when you bought your parking ticket.

Maids Moreton lies just a mile north of Buckingham, on the Towcester road, and for all practical purposes it is really a suburb of the town. It seems somewhat scandalous to admit this, and of course it's not how some 'villagers' in Maids

Moreton see things, no matter all the evidence to the contrary. Most people only know of a place called Maids Moreton because Buckingham Rugby Union Football Club is situated there (and therefore the two get verbally and descriptively integrated as one), along with a good old-fashioned thatched-roof pub called the Wheatsheaf, which has a cosy inglenook fire inside and a beer garden outside. Maids Moreton has been swallowed up by Buckingham, in much the same way that one day Buckingham will be swallowed up by Milton Keynes. So, despite what some might claim, usually in the Wheatsheaf, Maids Moreton doesn't really have a separate identity from Buckingham, even if it did make for better newspaper copy in the aftermath of Peter's murder, to depict it as a functioning village like something in *Midsomer Murders*.

I think that one final observation about Buckingham is worth mentioning. The wealth of its inhabitants, and the rather well-off student population, is reflected in a surprising number of decent places to eat, both in and around the town, as the *Sunday Times* restaurant critic A. A. Gill, quoted at the start of the chapter, was to discover. He also tells a couple of stories that are helpful in understanding Buckingham's civic and political culture.

*

Adrian Anthony Gill, who died in 2016, was a recovering alcoholic and failed artist who found fame as a writer and critic. When Gill came to Buckingham in spring 2010, he was not actually there to review a restaurant, but was instead attempting to write a story about John Bercow, the town's MP and Speaker of the House of Commons, standing in the general election. It is a tradition that the Speaker is elected unopposed, although in 2010 Nigel Farage, a founding member of UKIP, who had been its leader between 2006 and 2009, decided to stand against Bercow, as did a number of independent candidates. One of these was John Stevens, who had organised for a man dressed as a dolphin to follow Bercow around the hustings. The dolphin – known as Flipper – was an allusion to the fact that Bercow had 'flipped' his second home, a practice which was perfectly legal but was seen as immoral and part of the expenses scandal that had engulfed parliament between 2009 and 2010.

Bercow denied Gill an interview, claiming that he would only speak to local journalists. So Gill got employed for the day by the *Bucks Free Press*, although that ruse didn't impress Bercow, who continued to deny Gill access. As a consequence, Gill had to make do with interviewing Farage and several of the independents, including Stevens.

Of course, the story became about Farage and his clearly calculated decision to stand in the constituency, which must have been in part based on a reading of Buckingham's culture and history, and perhaps Bercow's unpopularity. The type of background I have described can make the town appear, at first sight, as 'naturally conservative'. In other words, classic UKIP territory, although that would be to misread the much more pragmatic history and culture of the town and the surrounding villages which made up the constituency. It could, after all, support the King or the Parliamentarians during the Civil War and so suspend its political inclination to make a much more pragmatic practical calculation. It had elected John Bercow, but it had also happily elected Robert Maxwell as a Labour MP in 1964.

As only outsiders can really do, Gill set the scene with great insight, humour and rather movingly in his article, which appeared under the title 'The Battle of the Non Speakers' in April 2010. He described how

Buckingham is the pivot of the nation. You either despise its beady probity with a Molotov-lobbing loathing, or tearfully worship it as a symbol of this sceptred isle that stands for Spitfires and Stannah stairlifts, pewter tankards, property booms and knowing your place. It is England's Kosovo.

As he walked with Farage through the town, he observed how everyone seemed to like and respect Bercow – and how he'd 'never come across such consistent praise for a politician'. I know myself that Bercow was a regular speaker at the rugby club, where he would be greeted with cries of 'stand up', a good-hearted allusion to his (lack of) height, after he had risen to start his talk, and there is hardly a constituent who doesn't have a story about his willingness to come and open a fête or attend a school play, or who remembers him standing outside in the rain in the market square raising money for a local cause.

These personal memories of Bercow make his autobiography all the more disappointing. Published after he stood down as Speaker, *Unspeakable* makes no mention whatsoever of the constituency he represented for more than twenty years. We hear nothing about his preferred pub, local walks that he might have taken in the area with his family, or which was his favourite village. In fact if you have never visited Buckingham and want to know something about it, don't turn to Bercow's book as you will learn absolutely nothing about the place. He might as well have been MP for the Moon.

A. A. Gill never got to meet Bercow (and his attempt to do so did not feature in *Unspeakable*), but he was clearly not impressed by his encounters with Farage. He described him as 'a man whose character was formed by a thousand snug bars', and that he 'has breath that could club a baby seal to death'.

A couple of weeks later, Gill's review of Halibut, one of the restaurants in the town, appeared in the *Sunday Times*. As he acknowledges, he had dined there because Zakima, the Nigerian co-owner, had grabbed him in the street as he was following Farage on the hustings, and she had begged him to come and eat in the restaurant that she owned with her sister and Sam, her partner. Gill described Zakima as 'beautifully very, very black. And while it's not wholly unknown in Buckingham ... it's rare'. He concluded that Halibut was 'a good restaurant, an exceptional one in Buckingham'. It was his observations about the town, however, that are perhaps more revealing, and capture the essence of the place.

Gill describes, in the quote that I use at the start of the chapter, how Buckingham really is in 'the green heart of England' and how this would be said with a 'moue of self-love [and] a treacly dose of self-pity'. Taking the restaurant review and his earlier article together, Gill characterises Buckingham as both a place with an obvious history that is important to understanding its culture: the self-love, but also the self-pity (that would be Aylesbury again!); nostalgia for a time that has been lost; wealth; and a future that has to be built on the practicalities of the present. Halibut, and food more generally, was for Gill part of that future, as exemplified in the story of Zakima and Sam. They had moved to Buckingham because their son played rugby, they liked the schools and they had wanted to bring him up in the countryside. As Gill described it,

> Zakima is so bright, enthusiastic, happy, balanced, productive and welcome – such a killing antidote to the grey fear and resentment of populist politics. All migrant stories are like this – all exceptional, all touching and brave. The migrant is counter safety and blandness, counter laissez faire and fear. It is the nature of new beginnings to hope and work hard.

A few days after his review of Halibut appeared, Bercow was re-elected as MP for Buckingham with nearly 50 per cent of the vote, although his overall share of the vote had been reduced by over 10 per cent. However, he didn't lose these votes to Farage. John Stevens and Flipper came second, with more than ten thousand votes (again not mentioned in *Unspeakable*), leaving Farage trailing in third place with 8410 votes. On the day of the election itself, Farage was involved in an accident when the two-seater plane that he had chartered to carry himself and a banner – 'Vote for your Country – Vote UKIP' – crashed on landing at the small airfield in Hinton-in-the-Hedges, after the banner had become caught in the plane's tail fin.

It is a wonderful metaphor and one that I would never have dreamed up myself.

Sadly there was no happy ending for Zakima and Sam. I knew both of them very well and ate regularly in Halibut, which would later change its name to Bucca in an attempt to attract more customers by nodding to the town's past. It didn't work, and they eventually had to close the restaurant. The restaurateurs who took it over serve Mexican food – it is now called Carnitas – and is run by an Asian chef and his Eastern European wife; I have breakfast there every Saturday morning with my friend Professor Michael Brookes, a forensic psychologist with whom I spend hours discussing the issues of the day.

However, there is something in what Gill says more generally, in the story of Halibut specifically, and of the personal stories of Zakima and Sam, that captures the authentic, oxymoronic culture of Buckingham. It is a pragmatic place rather than ideological; welcoming, if somewhat worried about being seen to be nosy; traditional, but still wanting to be thought of as important to the here and now; and rather self-satisfied, even if, all the time, mildly put out that it hasn't been given the credit for all that it has achieved in the past.

These themes would also emerge in my discussions with two of my friends who live in the town – one had been brought up in Maids Moreton and the other runs his business from an office there – and in what they said about Peter's murder. Their voices bring the issues I have been describing to life by making them truly local, rather than simply the observations of a talented journalist. And, unlike A. A. Gill, I didn't just want to describe and observe, but to understand and analyse, and there is no better way to do that than to listen to what people say, especially if those people can take you to the heart of the story, or open up those areas which, at first glance, seem confusing. What they'd describe allowed me to gain a deeper insight into the culture of Maids Moreton and both

Buckingham town and the university, and bring the murder and the questions that surround it much closer to home.

*

Ross and Julian, who I have always called Jules, are two of my oldest friends. Both are in their fifties, still fit and active. In rugby terms, Jules is a natural forward and, if Ross had actually played, he'd have been in the backs. The three of us first met on the touchline of a rugby pitch shouting instructions to our sons who, at the time, were seven years old. We would go on to stand on similar touchlines for the next eleven years, shouting different instructions as our boys grew older, bigger and, if I am honest (although Jules would never admit to this), better at rugby than we ever were. Quite apart from rugby, our sons initially went to the same school, although Jack – Jules's oldest boy – would go on to the Royal Latin, the town's historic grammar school, while Hugo and Ollie went to the independent Akeley Wood. The schools of our children and rugby meant that we had things in common and, over time, a deep bond of friendship developed from these common interests. We still see each other on a regular basis, at the rugby club and for a pint in the Wheatsheaf, usually on a Thursday night, at least until coronavirus took hold. At my suggestion we met up to discuss the culture of Buckingham, Maids Moreton and, of course, to talk about murder.

Jules moved to Maids Moreton in 1967, because his father got a job selling agricultural chemicals and so, at the age of ten, he found himself living in what he persists in calling a village and the rest of us describe simply as the edge of Buckingham. He would stay there until he moved away from home when he turned eighteen, and he now lives in another part of the town. Even so, he sees himself as belonging to the vanished place of Maids Moreton; he's an insider; and, despite all the evidence to the contrary, as a 'villager'. Ross, on the other hand, was born in Carlisle and brought up in Darlington. When he moved south for work with his family, he had to choose between setting up home in Milton Keynes, or in Buckingham. Buckingham won out, and he now runs his business from an office in Maids Moreton – chosen, he assures me, for the pragmatic reason that it is less than a mile from his home. He is therefore an outsider, even though he has lived in the area since 1999. Ross actively chose Buckingham, unlike Jules, who had the choice made for him. Ross made a conscious decision to come to live in the town, for himself and for his family. Why? 'It's a community,' he said to me, 'a bit like Goldilocks – not too big, not too small. Just right. The children say that their childhood was "vanilla": safe, predictable. They joke about it now, but isn't that better than having to be brought up in an environment with stabbings and shootings? Vanilla has a bad reputation, if you ask me!'

Jules and Ross also have different stories of how they made inroads into the community. Jules formed relationships through going to school in the town, and he still socialises with some of the people he met at that time, while Ross, at least initially, made connections through the relationships that his children formed after they went to school. 'It was the school at first and then the rugby club – of course – the Round Table for the business, and now Jane [his wife] rides and so we have begun to know people through that interest too. It's a friendly place.' Both Ross and Jules thought that culture of schools and education dominated the town and, more than that, Ross believed that education had now actually come to define Buckingham and the people who lived there: 'It's like a San Andreas Fault under the surface. You are defined by where you went to school – the Latin, Akeley or Stowe.'

Jules agreed with this, but he had a slightly different take on the culture of education within the town, as he and his family had moved to Buckingham before the university had been established. 'For many of the older people living here,' he said, 'there's not a lot of love for the university, or for the students. It's not so much about race – a lot of the students are black or Asian – it is just that neither the students, nor the university, seem to have contributed anything to the town and its development. All UB seems to have done is push up house prices and that's meant that a lot of the younger locals have had to move away.' Jules also felt that the demographic of Buckingham was changing, with more people living in the town and its suburbs, partly through the increase of social housing in the area. He felt that these changes meant that there were more people coming into the town that he no longer knew. 'I used to be able to go into any pub and know somebody drinking at the bar, but not now.' Ross disagreed, reminding Jules that he originated from Carlisle and had been brought up in Darlington, and therefore could state quite categorically that 'Buckingham is not a working-class town'.

I'd have to agree with Ross, but their observations reminded me of one of my early anonymous interviewees, who described Buckingham as being like 'Middle England in flux' – the culture was changing, but deep down Buckingham was still very much 'a red chinos town'. It was a metaphor about class and education, as much as it was about fashion. This interviewee thought that it was incredible that 'the principal place for buying clothes is still an old-fashioned tailor's shop in the town'. My interviewee suggested that you should just hang out at the Royal Latin, and 'that's where you'll find the highest percentage of red chinos. Substitute any *Monty Python* names here – it's where they all go to meet each other.'

I was intrigued by Ross's observation about education being like the San Andreas Fault within the town's culture. The San Andreas Fault runs for approximately 1200 kilometres beneath California and forms the tectonic boundary between the Pacific plate and the North American plate; the shifting movements of those plates were the cause of the 1906 San Francisco earthquake, in which nearly three thousand people lost their lives. In other words, those things, to paraphrase Freud, which are unseen and beneath the surface can have a dramatic impact on how lives are lived above ground. What was the San Andreas Fault of Middle England? At a more immediate level, Ross's reflection also offered me an opportunity to ask more difficult and direct questions which didn't often crop up in our normal Thursday-night meetings.

Ross, for example, had described how his children thought of Buckingham as 'vanilla', and yet it was here that a man had been slowly groomed over five years and horrifically murdered – and no one had seemed to notice. It was a friendly place, so why had no one intervened? Jules responded:

It's a village – Maids Moreton – that respects people's privacy; respects people's space. They don't gossip, or poke their noses into other people's business. And, if I am being honest, even if I didn't really know who they were, I thought of Field and Peter as outsiders to Maids Moreton. I don't mean in a villagers with pitchforks sort of way, but they really weren't considered to be from Maids Moreton, or even Buckingham. I hardly knew anything about them.

Jules's views are of interest here, and get us to the heart of how the murder could have taken place in plain sight. My friends' assessments and personal histories also reveal how people truly *become* part of a community, as opposed to simply *living* in a community. This implies that neither Peter nor Field had ever become part of a wider network; Peter didn't have a child, and never stood on the rugby touchline shouting instructions at them alongside other parents. Of course, Peter did teach at Stowe, but that is very different from being a parent – he didn't chat casually with the other parents about their respective kids, and arrange to have coffee together. These banal and seemingly trivial matters are the stuff that really does make community; they are the social glue that binds one individual to another.

Both Peter and Field were publicly associated with the university, and the town, as Jules put it, didn't have 'a lot of the love' either for UB or for the students. A local culture that respected people's space and privacy meant that no one wanted to 'poke their noses' into their business, even if that business was murder.

I wondered if Peter's and Field's sexuality would have raised any red flags. Did either Ross or Jules know anyone in the town who was openly gay? They looked incredulously at each other and replied, almost in unison, 'Yes!'

'You've got to remember,' Jules said, 'the rugby club has a

very inclusive and diverse group of people who play and many of the Swans [the female side] are in same-sex relationships.' Ross also felt that 'it's not an issue at all. We've had some gay couples who are out in the town for over a decade.'

It seems, then, the passive, toxic culture of 'Middle England in flux' could look past sexuality and the scandalous notion that an older man was living with a much younger male companion, and simply say, 'Well, that's their business'. No 'pitchforks', as Jules describes, or running them out of the village, but instead a respectful, arms-length tolerance; acceptance, perhaps with what A. A. Gill described as a 'tumpty-tum smirk', but not quite inclusion.

*

Ross and Jules had something else in common that was relevant to the case. Both had lost their fathers in the preceding year, and Jules's dad had died in the Red House Nursing Home in Maids Moreton. Field had been working there as a carer since 2013, after completing his MA. As he would describe it on his CV, he worked in the nursing home 'providing and coordinating end-of-life care in a dementia specialist unit'. He made it all sound very skilled and professional; capable and clinical. I knew that this was challenging territory, but I was keen to hear my friends' thoughts about their elderly parents, and how they had been able to include them in their lives. How could they, and we more generally as a society, better integrate the elderly into everyday culture?

But first there was a surprise.

I started to explain that Field had been working at the Red House Nursing Home and that the police had discovered that he had a list of a hundred largely elderly people, whom he thought might be useful to him. The colour drained from Jules's face.

'I never knew that,' he said.

'You mean the list?' I replied.

'No. That he'd been working at Red House. It's a bit of a shock. That's where my father was, and he had dementia.' Jules asked the next and obvious question: was his father on that list?

I had no idea, as the police have never released many details beyond the fact that Field's own parents were on it, plus one or two other named individuals, and so I suggested that he should contact Thames Valley Police if he wanted more information. Jules was quiet for a moment and then, as if remembering some painful, subconscious details, said:

Dad had dementia, and his room was on the top floor, in a far corner, and so he was rather isolated from the care staff who were invariably in the day room with the active and not the bed-ridden residents, or they were shut away on the lower floor. I could occasionally sit with him for up to an hour without seeing another soul. If I could have been in his room for that length of time – undetected – then so could others. Looking back, I suppose that makes him vulnerable, and opens up possibilities for people like Field to abuse him.

I tried to reassure Jules as best as I could but, of course, what he was sharing was no doubt a story that could have been told by scores of other sons and daughters about their fathers or mothers in care homes. I was reminded of Harold Shipman, described by many of his patients as a 'trusted, old-fashioned local GP', but who abused that trust on the visits he made to their homes where he would quietly kill them. Who noticed? No one, until it was too late. What's perhaps worse is the thought that many of the families of his patients must have believed he had been doing a good job, and so were grateful to him. Grateful for the murderer, who was able to visit when they could not.

Jules's father had been cared for less than a mile from their family home where they had moved to in the 1960s, but Ross's father had lived in Darlington all his life, and inevitably some of the care arrangements had fallen to family members who lived closer. 'The long and the short of it,' said Ross, 'is that dementia means you lose them twice. First you lose them when their understanding goes and they don't know who you are any more, and then you lose them when they die.' Perhaps reflecting on the sombre mood that had descended on our evening, Ross added that the reality of having lost both of his parents had created for him a sense of 'cosmic awareness'. As he said this, both he and Jules laughed, puncturing the solemn tone. We were laughing in the face of death. It was getting too serious, and I knew that rugby always lightened the mood.

I thought that the rugby club had a very good approach to accommodating older people, I said, and that I'd seen all ages – from eight to eighty and beyond – mixing quite happily. There was even a rather elaborate bench beside the pitch, that had been erected to commemorate an old club member, which was now where other older members often sit. Over time, a shelter had been built to cover the bench, affording some protection from the weather. That seemed like a very practical way for the club to demonstrate that older people were valued.

At times it was a bit like a rugby conveyer belt: you come in to the club as minis at seven or eight, play in the various age groups, go off to university, play for one of the senior teams, become a vice-president, and then slowly but surely find yourself sitting on that bench. Jules warmed to my rugby theme, but also corrected me about what I had said:

It's not about 'accommodating' older people in the club. That doesn't capture what the culture is all about. Older people are simply accepted as part of what the club is – they are ex-players, ex-committee members and vice-presidents. I suppose it's about respect; I like that. I know that some of the older people wouldn't really have a social life without the club. They get picked up, given a pint and then taken home again after the game. You might think that the bench is a bit morbid; a bit ghostly. But I know that one day that will be my future too, with my sons looking after me and my grandsons and my granddaughters. It feels right. It feels safe. I wouldn't want it any other way.

Perhaps this 'simply being accepted' is a feature of the sport. After all, rugby relies on people of all shapes and sizes, with very different abilities and skills from one another to make a team. The shape and skillset of a prop is vastly different from those who will play in the backs but both are needed if the team is to be successful.

This seemed as good a conclusion to our conversation about getting older as any. The rugby club had fashioned a culture that saw the young and the old as equally important. I wondered why this would happen, and whether there was something about the game itself that might have created this type of culture. I said to Jules that I wanted an invitation the next time there was a lunch at the club, so I could chat about all of this with some of the older members. He readily agreed, although the pandemic has put paid to any lunch meetings at the club.

*

Neither Peter nor Field were interested in rugby, which perhaps helps to explain why I hardly knew them, and had only met Peter in passing. So, to understand them better I instead chose to rely on the records that they both left, and their common interest – literature – in order to build up a picture of their lives. I could also infer a great deal about their relationship from the murder itself, and later Field's behaviour in court. Of course, as I have described, there are difficulties with prioritising these sources and I worried that they might not offer me the full picture of how Peter was groomed, and how Field almost got away with his murder. I still wanted to understand the methods that Field had used to groom Peter, and others in the town, and why Peter had been so vulnerable to Field's 'snake talk'. Why was the town so happy to collude with what Field said? And how had Field's lies eventually been uncovered?

Last orders was called, and Jules and Ross looked at me expectantly.

I knew what I had to do. I put down my pen and made my way to the bar. We didn't realise it at the time, but it would be several months before we would be able to meet up again in a pub for a drink.

CHAPTER FIVE

Grooming

'The process by which a sexual predator gains
control over his victim'

BRENT TURVEY,
*Criminal Profiling: An Introduction
to Behavioral Evidence Analysis*

I watched as an elderly man, hunched precariously over two wooden sticks, walked very slowly, step by careful step, up the market square. He was wearing an overcoat to protect him from a bitter autumnal wind, although he didn't have a hat, a scarf, or even a pair of gloves. It was cold; really, really cold. Every few seconds he had to stop and gather his breath to summon up the energy to take another few paces, before he had to stop again, and then go through the same laborious process. It was painful to watch, and I can only imagine how difficult it must have been for him to keep going; every step he took seemed like a superhuman effort.

I didn't see anyone speak to him on his journey – the elderly man was quite alone, but I could tell that other people in the café were watching him too. Like a human CCTV system, we were all silently observing and recording what was happening; nothing was outside of our gaze, even if we might choose not to speak about it.

Jack, one of the waiters, who'd dropped out of university the previous year, brought over the two poached eggs on sourdough that I had ordered, and put them on the table in front of me. The week before he'd told me that he wanted to study forensic psychology, and so we'd had a brief conversation about what he'd encounter on an undergraduate psychology or criminology course.

Today I just smiled a silent 'thank you' and made a mental note to ask him later if he'd thought any further about his plans for the following year.

I broke the yolks of both eggs and glanced around the café. There were prints of old Buckingham on the walls and a mural dedicated to a Civil War battle that had been fought in the town, and another to some of its most famous residents, such as the Restoration novelist and playwright Mary Pix. It was warm and cosy inside, and so I was in no rush to leave; I sipped my flat white, and waited for the yolks to saturate the sourdough. I glanced out of the window again and watched the Union Jacks above Barclays Bank, and the British Heart Foundation and Scope charity shops rattle back and forth in the wind. There were also large ornamental poppies, nailed to the wooden pillars that marked out one of the town's more central car parks, to remind everyone that it was Remembrance Day.

We'd already had our two minutes of silence, 'lest we forget'.

I'm always slightly irritated by the nostalgia at the heart of that phrase, as I think that what happened in the past should make us think more carefully about what we need to do to create a better future. That's why thinking about the significance of Peter's murder more broadly is so important.

Beneath the flags, I noticed that the old man had made only a little progress.

Sitting in the café watching this painful journey unfold, I tried to make sense of how Peter's murder could have happened in plain sight, beyond what had been said to me by Ross and Jules. If nothing escaped our gaze, why didn't we notice that Peter was being groomed? We don't tend to think of grooming as something happening to the elderly, but Field was especially good at grooming the older people that he encountered, taking the time to really get to know them and their interests. The knowledge that Field gained allowed him to get close; really close, not just to Peter but to others.

Perhaps some did notice Field's grooming of Peter, but simply chose to ignore what they saw. 'It was their business,' I was repeatedly told. That estrangement played a crucial part in how Field manipulated and then controlled Peter and us.

Field had deliberately kept the community at arm's length, largely so he could control the narrative about what was happening to Peter. Thereafter everyone simply accepted the narrative that he was offering – spreading rumours that Peter was drinking too much and, a little later, that he had dementia. The idea that Peter was drinking himself to death is one of the reasons why the bottle of whisky was left on display beside Peter's body; it was a form of 'proof' about what Field had been saying. In a small town like Buckingham those rumours would have spread like wildfire. Field also filmed Peter, dazed and confused in his bed, so as to provide some sort of further evidence to these statements – should anyone have challenged him – and was able to alter the minutes of meetings at Stowe Parish Church, where they both worshipped, to include details of Peter's 'declining health'.

As all of this indicates, Field was accomplished as a perpetrator, and I tend to think so accomplished that he must have been developing different grooming tactics for almost all of his life. In his grooming of Peter, we can see a dizzying array of techniques on display: his professed love of literature, which created an immediate common interest between student and lecturer; his background in the church and his supposed faith again mirrored Peter's interests; and, as we would discover from his trial, Field was adept at using sex as a mechanism to get money, and to establish control.

In his dealings with Peter, he perfectly played the parts of both besotted suitor and committed Christian. He began by accompanying Peter to Stowe Parish Church, and would eventually embed himself there as a trusted member of the congregation. Once he had established that trust, he volunteered to take minutes in meetings, and took on a secretarial role to the Parochial Church Council (PCC). It was in this position that he was able to alter the minutes of meetings by adding comments about Peter's ill health, offering them as a reason for Peter's absence at church and elsewhere, and which served to further Peter's dependence on Field. That dependence only helped to isolate him further and cut him off from family – his brother Ian, his sister-in-law and their two sons, and his friends.

Field would later give Peter a dog that they called Kipling, which must also have bolstered that isolation. He would stay in to look after the dog, or fill his day walking Kipling, rather than attending concerts further afield. Separating Peter from his family and friends was crucial for Field's success.

After Field was eventually convicted, Peter's brother Ian and his wife Sue told *Good Morning Britain* in August 2020 they had believed what Field had told them about Peter – that he was sick, and required constant care – and were pleased that he was helping him. They were even grateful for Peter and Field's friendship because, as Ian described it, 'Peter had stopped teaching to write novels' and he felt that his brother 'missed being around young people'. When Field was first arrested, Sue thought the police had made a terrible mistake. Here was yet another echo of Shipman, whose patients had lined up, one after another, to defend him in the press, insisting he was a good doctor.

If Field was pretending to be sexually interested in Peter, he was very successful in his acting. He was persistent and skilful in his pursuit, even though Peter had always struggled to reconcile his homosexuality with his Christian beliefs. By 2014, Field had completely convinced Peter and, after visiting Samuel Taylor Coleridge's cottage together, like star-crossed lovers they agreed to formalise their relationship by having a betrothal ceremony at St Mary's, West Hampstead, with Glenn Gould's celebrated performance of Bach's Goldberg Variations playing hauntingly in the background. This was a strange choice of music, not least because one of the most famous cinematic uses of this Bach aria is in *The Silence of the Lambs*, when the serial killer Hannibal Lecter chews the face off one of his guards. I would also later remember a literary character – the deeply troubled and murderous Tom Ripley, created by Patricia Highsmith – who was also fond of playing the Goldberg Variations.

There were other eccentricities about the ceremony, which was conducted by Father Andrew Foreshew-Cain. For example, the pair exchanged penknives as a token of their love for each other and, whilst these keepsakes must have had significance for them, exchanging knives seems to me to be very strange. I have never really understood what all of this might have signified, but it was undoubtedly part of their ritual of commitment to each other and therefore an outcome of Field's grooming of Peter. Clearly a ring worn on the fourth finger of the left hand is the sign of an eternal union between two people, whereas a knife seems to symbolise something altogether different. Knives are sharp – they cut, maim and disfigure, and can sometimes be wielded as weapons to kill. Perhaps it was the cutting that was important; both had been known for their 'cutting remarks' in the past. And killing with a knife is very different from shooting someone. With a knife you have to get close to your victim. Of course when knives cut through flesh, blood is spilled and perhaps even exchanged and this can sometimes be done deliberately so as to become 'blood brothers'.

The music and the penknives were clearly deliberate choices that Field and Peter made. Even if I cannot determine categorically their significance, they do seem to add a subtext of drama, danger and perhaps even sadism to the event and I suspect that it was Field, rather than Peter, who had made the suggestions. After all, it is clear from what Peter wrote about their betrothal ceremony that he felt it was 'a blessed day. God is good to me.

Far more than I deserve.' He wrote that it was one of the 'happiest moments of my life. Gone are the fears of dying alone.'

Despite his faith, dying alone was clearly one of Peter's great fears, although his statement could also be read as a desire to form a relationship with someone else – he didn't want to live alone. Sadly, it would appear that his wish not to die alone was granted, as Field was present at the very end.

As Field's control over Peter intensified, he started to suggest to Peter and to other people that Peter had dementia, which is an umbrella term for a range of progressive conditions that affect the brain. Dementia can often be accompanied by a deterioration in memory, and the inability to perform simple, everyday tasks. Sometimes people with dementia will struggle to remember the names of their family and friends, and might misplace things on a regular basis. They will sometimes be forgetful and confused, and find it difficult to use the right words to describe common situations.

We now know that Peter's 'dementia' was merely the result of a sustained period of Field drugging him that had begun in January 2015. In that same month, Field had enrolled on his PhD at UB. I get the impression that the timing was not coincidental. Quite apart from beginning his doctoral studies, it had been a busy and somewhat complicated twelve months in Field's life. Not only had he set up a publishing company called Farquhar Studies with Martyn Smith, one of his friends from university, but he had also become secretary to the PCC at Stowe Parish Church and was juggling at least three relationships: with Peter; with a young woman called Lara Busby, whom he had first started to date in 2012; and with his PhD supervisor, Dr Setara Pracha.

He was also using the Grindr app to meet men. A number of murders have been associated with Grindr – for example, in 2016 the serial killer Stephen Port was convicted of killing four men he had met through the app. Port would arrange to meet up with his targets and then give them overdoses of the drug GHB. He was motivated by a desire for power and control over his victims. Gerald Matovu, Port's drug dealer, was a prolific thief, and like Port, he would also target victims via Grindr. He used GHB to render these victims unconscious so that he could steal their possessions, although as his offending career progressed, Matovu turned to murder. One such victim was Eric Michels, who Matovu killed in 2018.

I wonder to what extent Field's use of Grindr and the drugs that are used by some gay men also crossed over into the drugs that he would use on Peter. In August 2015, for example, a launch for Peter's book *A Wide Wide Sea* had been arranged at Stowe School. It did not go well and we now know that Peter's shambolic, rambling appearance at his book launch was the result of Field having drugged him with 2C-B. This is a designer psychedelic drug, somewhat similar to LSD, which was created in the 1970s. It is also sold as an aphrodisiac, under the trade name Erox, as it increases sexual interest and pleasure, and has the rather obvious 'wink-wink' street names of Eve, Nexus, Performax and Venus. It is illegal in the UK but available on the internet, and it's possible that Field had used the drug to sexually abuse Peter without him ever realising. What is certain is that some people using the drug can experience frightening visual hallucinations, with the effects lasting between two and four hours.

*

At its simplest, the motive behind all of this grooming seems to have been financial. In that sense, Field was similar to Kemi Adeyoola, who stabbed her former neighbour, eighty-four-year-old Ann Mendel, to death in 2005, as a 'practice run' to kill elderly women in the hope of raising £3 million – a motive she revealed in a 'murder manual' she wrote in prison. Field used different tactics from Adeyoola and instead tricked Peter into altering his will. Field was motivated by greed – the second of the seven deadly sins, which comes after pride and before lust, envy, gluttony, wrath and sloth. As a self-proclaimed Christian, Field would know that a pursuit of wealth above all other things is to ignore the realm of the spiritual. In the Bible, Greed is also sometimes called 'avarice' and 'covetousness', and, if you believe in that sort of thing, the greedy person's punishment in Hell is to be boiled in oil.

Along with drugging Peter, Field also engaged in a sustained period of 'gaslighting' him, which was yet another technique in his arsenal of grooming tactics. I don't know how the gaslighter might be punished in Hell, but I do know that the term comes from a 1938 play called *Gas Light*, by the British playwright and novelist Patrick Hamilton, which was also later made into a film directed by Thorold Dickinson. This in turn was remade in 1944, directed by George Cukor and starring Ingrid Bergman, who won an Oscar for her performance. Set in a fog-bound London in 1880, the plot involves a murderous, domineering husband browbeating his somewhat timid wife into believing that she is simply imagining that the gas light in their house periodically dims, or that she can hear footsteps in the empty flat above their own. However, the gas does indeed dim, and the footsteps in the empty upstairs flat belong to her husband.

From these humble dramatic beginnings, gaslighting has come to mean a form of psychological torture. For example, Field would gaslight Peter by removing items from his home, only for them to reappear later 'in ridiculous places', leaving Peter feeling as if he were going crazy. We glimpse this gaslighting in a letter that Peter sent to his local GP, Dr Jonathan Pryce, in which he expresses confusion and fears he is losing his mind, and suggests that he had become King Lear, the Shakespearean character who progressively grows more insane as he doubts his own judgements and blinds himself to the truth. In another email summarising his symptoms, which he copied to Dr Pryce, Peter writes of one evening,

That dreadful night was spent with the support of two of my friends, Ben and Martyn, in the bathroom. I felt wretchedly ill but, far worse, were the illusions I kept seeing (e.g. mass of black insects on the carpet and climbing the radiator). While it was happening, I felt that I wanted to die, the experience was so unbearable. I persisted in hic-coughing. The other day when a passenger in a car, I saw brilliantly coloured horizontal downward sloping lights flash across the road (green, gold, white). Later I heard a loud gunshot which seemed to pass through my head. Neither of the other two people in the room heard it. It was another illusion.

Field merely suggested to all and sundry, especially at Stowe Parish Church, that these were all symptoms of Peter's dementia and alcoholism. His explanation was therefore both specific and yet vague enough to withstand any deep probing, and I certainly spoke with a couple of Peter's friends who insisted that they had challenged the idea that Peter had become an alcoholic. When that had happened, they explained that Field merely switched the conversation on to dementia.

The hallucinations that Peter experienced were clearly the result of combining the medication his doctor had prescribed for him, the drugs that Field was giving him surreptitiously, and the alcohol Peter was drinking. These hallucinations were a deliberate by-product of the mechanics of the murder and one that must have given Field a great deal of satisfaction.

Historically, we have thought of murderers as being 'act' or 'process' focused. Put simply, this means that some murderers are merely interested in the death of their victim, and so they kill quickly and without fuss. What they are seeking to achieve is the death of the person they have targeted. On the other hand, a process-focused killer is much more likely to prolong the experience of their victim's agony. Such a killer gains great pleasure from watching his victim's suffering, and often such a killer will be interested in sadism. He will also take 'trophies', such as photographs of his victim, or perhaps a piece of clothing or jewellery to remind him of what he has done after his victim has died. Field had control of Peter's novels as his trophy, as well as his house – before it was sold – his other writings and the films of Peter that he had made. He also had the penknife that they had exchanged in their betrothal ceremony. Trophies are often used as part of the killer's masturbatory fantasies to relive the murder after it has taken place.

Field would seem to fall in the process-focused category, and so he must have enjoyed watching Peter's 'declining health', while all the time knowing what was actually causing his illness.

Field would collect trophies from his other victims too. After Field was finished with Peter, he would go on to target his neighbour, the eighty-one-year-old retired teacher Ann Moore-Martin. As with Peter, Field used Ann's religious beliefs to persuade her that God intended them to be together. He began a sexual relationship with her and was soon defrauding her of her money, whilst all the time declaring his undying love. He claimed that he needed a new car, and so Ann gave him £4400, and later £27,000 in the belief that this was to help Field's brother Tom, who he claimed needed the money to buy a kidney dialysis machine. In July 2016 Field gave Ann a large photograph of himself with the words 'I am always with you' inscribed around the edge.

The grooming continued and his behaviour evolved, with 'automatic writing' – sometimes called 'psychography', or 'spirit writing' – appearing on her mirrors. Field even persuaded the elderly woman to perform oral sex, while all the time filming the encounter on his mobile phone, perhaps as a way to control her, or possibly because he was just so narcissistic that it gave him pleasure to watch himself. Taking the video is also a grooming tactic, and could just as easily have served as part of an effort to gain control over her once they had become close. Who might he have threatened to show the video to, if things didn't develop as he wished?

As I have suggested, it is also perfectly possible that Field really was a gerontophile, and so gained sexual pleasure from having sex with the elderly. He would not be the first murderer to target the elderly in this way. The little-known serial killer Kenneth Erskine was undoubtedly a gerontophile. Sometimes called the Stockwell Strangler, Erskine targeted elderly men and women in the summer of 1986, to rob, rape, sodomise and then kill. His first victim was seventy-eight-year-old Nancy Emms, whom he raped and then strangled. He went on to kill at least another six elderly people – both men and women – before he was finally caught. Erskine was not so much concerned about the gender of his victims, only that they were elderly. It is also interesting to note that, like Peter, Nancy's death was initially believed to have been due to natural causes and was recorded as such on her death certificate. It was only when her home help noticed that the TV was missing from her flat that a post-mortem was conducted, revealing the true cause of death.

The opposite of a gerontophile is a gerontophobe. Another little-known British serial killer, the 'cul-de-sac killer' Stephen Akinmurele, hated old people and murdered his five elderly victims between 1995 and 1998. Akinmurele is suspected of at least two other murders. He committed suicide in prison in Manchester just weeks before his trial was due to start in 1999, and that is perhaps why Akinmurele's case is so rarely discussed.

Akinmurele and Erskine were schizophrenics and had long histories of serious mental health problems. As a result of Erskine's diminished responsibility, his murder convictions were eventually reduced on appeal to manslaughter. Field, on the other hand, had no such issues – he was legally responsible for his actions – and seems to have also rather enjoyed toying with the police about his role in Peter's murder. After the deaths of Peter and of Ann, he'd even preached a sermon on the theme of 'Thou Shalt Not Kill' at his father's church – a recording of which was on the church's website for a time. In other words, as the net was slowly being tightened around him Field seems to have revelled in trying to keep all of his various plates spinning by maintaining a public pretence of being a committed Christian and a serious scholar.

That thought reminded me of Patricia Highsmith's 1955 psychological thriller *The Talented Mr Ripley*, which contains one of the most accurately drawn portraits of a murderous psychopath I have ever encountered in literature. Tom Ripley's talent was grooming people too; of being able to get close – really close, so that he could even impersonate their voice and mannerisms – before he'd end their lives. I started to think of Field as being like a less talented Ripley, even if I found it difficult to be certain if he had studied the book under Peter during his time at the University of Buckingham. 'Less talented' because, of course, Ripley never got caught.

*

Patricia Highsmith could not be described as an easy interviewee. I watched or listened to her three times: first, being interviewed by Mavis Nicholson in 1978, on Thames Television's *Good Afternoon*; then appearing on Channel 4's provocative discussion programme *After Dark* a decade later in 1988; and, finally, talking with the crime writer Michael Dibdin at the Institute of Contemporary Arts (ICA) about the Ripley series in 1991. She seemed to warm to Nicholson best, while Dibdin, the creator of the Venice-born detective Aurelio Zen, had a particularly hard time of it, with each of his reasonable questions being batted back with a 'yes', a 'no', or a single-sentence reply dragged kicking and screaming out of the back of Highsmith's throat. She seemed to be almost spitting at Dibdin. It was so obviously awkward that I was glad only an audio version of their discussion has survived. She was even more extraordinary on *After Dark*, where she insensitively questioned a fellow guest called David Howden, whose daughter Tessa had been strangled in her bedroom by a local man called Gary Taken. As David described the scene that he had discovered in his daughter's bedroom on the morning after her murder, he said, 'Friends and neighbours had to go and clean that bedroom up. The stains and fingerprints. They had to take the carpet up, sandpaper the floor and get rid of the marks, buy a new carpet and put it down.'

It was harrowing to watch, but Highsmith merely leaned forward and asked the poor man, 'What kind of marks?'

Highsmith was born in Texas in 1921, and her parents divorced just weeks before her birth. As a young girl she was a voracious reader and was particularly fond of Dr Karl Menninger's *The Human Mind*, which was published in 1930. This was a very popular, detailed account of 'deviant behaviour', which no doubt influenced Highsmith's writing. Menninger, who would go on to become president of the American Psychoanalytical Association, used the book to explain complex psychological problems, in much the same way that Oliver Sacks would later use his books to explain intricate neurological problems. Highsmith enrolled at Barnard College in New York in 1938, where she studied English literature. Her first novel, *Strangers on a Train*, was published in 1950, and made into a film by Alfred Hitchcock the following year. She died in 1995, at her home in Switzerland; she always preferred the Old World to the New, where her books sold well and where she became something of a celebrity.

Highsmith is often described as a crime writer. This seems a rather superficial way of capturing what her novels are concerned with; rather, they slowly seduce the reader into accepting the chaotic, illogical and irrational as normal. In her private journals she wrote that she thought that a 'man would snuff out his existence rather than endure a life which was rational, determined, planned and predicted' and there-fore, in the words of Andrew Wilson, although also adopting the observation of the political philosopher Hannah Arendt, 'she documents the banality of evil'. To state the obvious, Highsmith is not writing conventional crime fiction; she's not writing whodunnits.

Like other existentialist writers, Highsmith was drawn to criminals and especially to murderers. In her journal she noted that 'murder is a kind of making love, a kind of possess-ing' and Graham Greene, one of her greatest admirers, and whom Peter had also taught Field about at UB, considered her 'the poet of apprehension', one who had created 'a world without moral endings'.

Her most extraordinary creation is Tom Ripley, who would feature in five of her twenty-two novels. Andrew Wilson describes Ripley as 'a cold-blooded killer with a taste for the finer things in life. He paints and sketches, plays Bach's Goldberg Variations, reads Schiller and Molière and is proud of his art collection. He kills, but is moved to tears at the sight of Keats's grave.' This is a useful description, and hints at how Thomas Harris's serial-killing connoisseur, Dr Hannibal

Lecter, had an obvious literary antecedent. We should also remember that the Goldberg Variations were played at Peter and Field's strange betrothal ceremony, where they had exchanged penknives. Here again we have a 'double': the apparent incompatibility of art and literature living cheek by jowl with murder.

Ripley is a psychopathic murderer who is never caught, and we slowly begin to hope that he succeeds; we take his side – we don't want him caught either, in much the same way that more recent audiences have rooted for the eponymous serial killer in *Dexter*. It could be argued that Highsmith's writing asks us to throw our moral compass aside or, at the very least, suspend our morality for the duration of the book. There is no trial, no judgment, and the killer does not get punished. In fact, the killer prospers. Dibdin wondered in his ICA interview if we are on Ripley's side because of his 'taste', although Highsmith gave that idea short shrift. 'Is [his] the lifestyle of a psychopath?' Dibden tried once more, to which Highsmith merely replied, 'Well, it isn't quite normal.'

When we first meet Tom Ripley, he's twenty-six years old, insecure and social-climbing. He hasn't yet got his art collection, or even a watch. He wants money, of course, but also better food, clothes, a car; his sexuality is ambiguous; he has energy, emotion and anger; he also wants to be better read, and tries to borrow a copy of Henry James's *The Ambassadors* as he sails from New York to Europe. It isn't available, so Ripley never actually reads the book. Essentially, he's a chameleon who will take on the identity of those people who surround him, to the extent that the 'real' Tom Ripley will disappear. As readers we know that we have to be careful about Tom, because there truly is a deadly difference between appearance and reality; a difference between what the other characters in the novel see, and what we as readers know.

In *The Talented Mr Ripley*, Tom has been hired by the wealthy Herbert Greenleaf to bring his estranged son Dickie back from Italy to the United States so that he can join the family firm. Tom falls in love with Dickie's lifestyle and more than a little in love with Dickie himself but, realising that he can never possess his love object – that he can never have Dickie – he kills him and assumes his identity. Murder is a way of possessing what he desires and of solving his problems; it is also a perverse form of love.

Even as he is sailing to Europe, Tom starts playing with his identity. 'He began to play a role on the ship,' Highsmith writes, 'that of a serious young man with a serious job ahead of him. He was courteous, poised, civilized and preoccupied.' Like Nick Guest in *The Line of Beauty*, who moves in with the Feddens, Tom moves in with Dickie, and three times a week takes Italian lessons in the hope of developing his language skills. He's going to sound like Dickie too. Quite quickly he becomes jealous of Dickie's American girlfriend Marge, who in turn suspects that Tom is gay, which Tom angrily denies. This leads to one of the most interesting passages in the book, which Dibdin described at the ICA as 'the dressing-up scene':

He went upstairs to Dickie's room and paced around for a few moments [...] he jerked Dickie's closet door open and looked in. There was a freshly pressed, new-looking grey flannel suit that he had never seen Dickie wearing. Tom took it out. He took off his knee-length shorts and put on

116

the grey flannel trousers. He put on a pair of Dickie's shoes. Then he opened the bottom drawer of the chest and took out a clean blue-and-white striped tie.

Tom continues to try on Dickie's clothes, parts his hair in the same way as Dickie parts his, and then, looking at himself in the mirror and mimicking Dickie's higher-pitched voice, says, 'Marge, you understand that I *don't* love you.' He then grabs the air as if he was squeezing Marge's throat, shaking and twisting her until she lay dead on the floor. 'You know why I had to do that . . . you were interfering between Tom and me – No, not that! But there *is* a bond between us.' As he does all of this, Dickie catches him dressed in his clothes.

This edgily written and extraordinary powerful scene, with Tom not only wearing Dickie's clothes but also mimicking his voice, mirrors what will happen later in the book, and offers us the first glimpse of Tom's identity beginning to dissolve into Dickie's. Of course, this new identity wasn't his either; he was merely playing a role, even if he played it well. His appearance may have been convincing, but it wasn't real, or trustworthy; it was an act.

What's even more frightening to consider is that in real life, as opposed to just between the pages of a book, there are many Tom Ripleys: walking the streets, managing companies, attending academic seminars – all playing their parts well, even if they're actually inauthentic and hollow to the core. Field was one of those Ripleys.

As I continued my research, I wondered to what extent Field was also dressing up in the mirror, mimicking the voices of those he admired and who surrounded him, and all the time shuffling off his own identity and becoming someone else. Like Ripley, was Field also insecure and social-climbing, eager for a life that better fitted with who he thought he was, or wanted to become? At school and university he seemed to want to be an academic, and so he had to learn his lines so as to be able to play the part, but to what extent was this desire genuine, or merely part of an elaborate game, was the question on my mind. He also projected a specific identity at Stowe Parish Church: as a man of faith, who wanted to be ordained. Of course murder would also be central in his story, and while Field didn't want to 'become' Peter Farquhar, as Tom Ripley had wanted to become Dickie Greenleaf, killing was a way of possessing, of owning Peter and, more instrumentally, gaining access to his home and to his money. Like Ripley, he could love literature and art, appreciate classical and popular music, and yet still be capable of murder.

Field's behaviour was escalating, getting more and more out of control. Where would it end? He was becoming involved with too many people, and just as embedded in Stowe Parish Church as he was at the university. As he wrote in one of his chat logs, 'I'm gonna becoe [sic] a vicar and shit just because I can outmanoeuvre the church.' Could he manage to keep all of these personal and institutional plates spinning at the same time? Surely this created competing demands that needed to be carefully managed. Field didn't seem to think that this was a problem. As he saw things, he was cleverer than every-one else – he could outmanoeuvre those that he needed to convince – but he also seemed to believe that the parts he was playing were authentic, and so if he didn't question what he was doing, why would anyone doubt him?

And so what if an occasional plate fell crashing to floor? There were lots more that he could find to replace them. After Peter he had Ann, he started a relationship with his supervisor Setara Pracha, he had the congregation, and the elderly people at the care home in which he worked. Field was a skilled offender, with his sights set on many more victims after he had killed off poor Peter.

*

Peter's health continued to decline. Concerns about his condition meant a couple of admissions to hospital in Milton Keynes and at Stoke Mandeville for brain scans, although the results were normal. During this period he also saw a number of doctors at the Swan Practice – the GP surgery in Buckingham. He regularly complained about tiredness, forgetfulness, falling down and being unable to get back up again, and just generally feeling 'wretchedly ill'. He wrote to Dr Pryce on 3 September 2015, summarising his health issues:

> Since the middle of June, I have made mistakes which I would not normally have made: decline in handwriting, computer errors, regularly falling asleep in front of the T.V. but also during concerts, operas, cinema and theatre and as a passenger in cars. I have felt very tired. I have confused dates. I forget names of people and places. My sense of balance has been uncertain. Formerly a voracious reader, I have not read a book for some time.

This last issue, for a man so obviously in love with literature, must have been especially exasperating, and no doubt it gave Field – the process-focused killer – tremendous satisfaction.

After all, he was robbing Peter of his great love and one of the constants in his life.

Peter also described an incident on 29 June, when he had a heavy fall in the bathroom, which resulted in his cutting his face. An ambulance had to be called by 'my friend Ben Field'. He was taken to hospital in Milton Keynes where he was 'thoroughly examined', and where it was suggested that he might have low blood pressure and a urinary tract infection. While a course of antibiotics cleared up the UTI, Peter described how he had woken up on Tuesday 27 July feeling sick and unsteady, and that he did not make any sense when he was talking to people. 'Apparently,' he wrote, 'at one stage, I unaccountably reverted to my second language, German, speaking fluently but with only one other person in the room understanding what I was saying.' His condition worsened during the rest of the day. Peter did acknowledge that there were periods when 'I felt almost back to normal', but that 'quite suddenly, the illness strikes again one way or another'. When that happened, his speech became slurred and his memory failed him. He finished by saying, 'I spend ages looking for items I mislay, only for them to be found in ridiculous places.'

There was something else that Peter hadn't fully described in his summary to Dr Pryce, but which is worth noting and which I alluded to: 'the worst day of my life', as he put it to a friend, which had occurred the previous month, on the day of his book launch for *A Wide Wide Sea* in the grand Marble Hall at Stowe School.

A Wide Wide Sea was a coming of age story that he had written many years before, but which had failed to find a publisher. This time the book was not going to be self-published by

AuthorHouse, but by Farquhar Studies Ltd, the company set up by Field and Smith. Its registered office was 3 Manor Park, Maids Moreton – Peter's address, where Field was also living, although he gave his address on the incorporation documents as 'Post Room, Hunter Street' and described himself as a 'lecturer', even if he was simply taking some undergraduate seminars alongside his PhD. Ever the narcissist, it must have given him great satisfaction to write 'lecturer'.

Smith gave his address as 'The Porter's Lodge, University of Buckingham' and he described himself as a 'writer/researcher', making no mention of his part-time work – being a magician. Martyn Smith will play a somewhat tertiary role in this case, although he would be charged together with Field for the murder of Peter and conspiracy to murder Ann Moore-Martin, as well as multiple counts of fraud and one burglary. However, he was acquitted of all charges.

Farquhar Studies Ltd would publish *A Wide Wide Sea*, which was dedicated to both Field and Smith. It is now very difficult to access.

We know a little of Field and Smith's plans for Farquhar Studies Ltd beyond their publication of *A Wide Wide Sea* because they emailed a number of people saying that they wanted to make a documentary about Peter, which was to be called 'The Moral of the Story: The Literature of Peter Farquhar'. Smith explained that 'we are currently developing a documentary about the life and work of Peter Farquhar, and would be deeply grateful for any help that you can offer most especially if you would be willing to be interviewed on camera'. Peter seems to have endorsed this idea and he also emailed (as far as it can be ascertained) his friends, stating 'I understand that two of my former students at Buckingham University, Ben Field and Martyn Smith, have already written to you, flattering me immensely by planning to run a short documentary of me on television about my novel writing and as a teacher.' Of course, having Peter's validation would also have encouraged his friends to have contributed to Field and Smith's plans.

In reality, this was merely a more corporate and very public version of what Field was doing privately: he was using Peter.

So, in July 2015, Field and Smith were to act as his publishers, and like all good publishers they had arranged various promotional events for the book. As I have described, these events were to start with a book launch.

It was a disaster, although that is perhaps exactly what Field had wanted. Here was public proof of what he had been saying privately and evidence, should it be necessary, that Peter really was 'losing it'. It also served to humiliate him in front of his friends and in the school where he had once been Head of English. Like the music chosen at their betrothal ceremony and the exchange of penknives, the choice of venue for the launch was likely to have been a carefully considered step in Field's choreography of the murder.

When he arrived with Field, Peter looked flushed and was visibly shaking, but not from excitement. He struggled to remember people's names, even those of friends who he had known for many years. Peter found it almost impossible to sign the books that people bought. It was very clear that, in the words of one of the attendees I interviewed, 'Peter wasn't himself. He looked awful and was, sad to say, falling apart in front of my eyes. I thought that he was ill, or drunk, or both.

Even when I spoke to him he made no sense. He spoke gibberish really. I left quite quickly after that; I just didn't want to be there. It was really awful. It was the last time that I saw him.'

Two months later, Peter was dead. As he had always hoped, he didn't die alone. Field was by his side.

We now know that what happened to Peter wasn't an accident. But so successful had Field been in grooming us, and the various statutory bodies required to investigate deaths, that it would take some time before anyone realised that Peter had been murdered.

CHAPTER SIX

A Blueprint for Murder

'Writing fiction is the act of weaving a series of
lies to arrive at a greater truth'

KHALED HOSSEINI

On the evening of Sunday 25 October 2015, Field had
gone to the house that he shared with Peter in Maids
Moreton and given him Dalmane, the trade name for the drug
flurazepam, which is typically used to treat insomnia. It is
sometimes also branded as Dulmadorm, and works by slow-
ing brain activity to allow the individual to sleep. Depending
on the dosage, some people using flurazepam have still been
able to drive cars, make phone calls, or even have sex, but are
then unable to later remember anything at all about engaging in these activities. There are especially dangerous side
effects of taking the drug if you also use or abuse alcohol at
the same time, as this will increase the sedative effect of both
substances and will lead to a decreasing level of consciousness. The near-empty bottle of whisky that was found next to

Peter's body is therefore a clue to what happened, although we do not know if Peter willingly took the Dalmane, was tricked into doing so, or if Field simply surreptitiously crushed some of the drug into his drink.

It is also likely that, at the very end, Field suffocated Peter with one of the cushions from the sofa, just to make certain that he was dead.

As if all of this wasn't bad enough, something even more appalling was still to be revealed.

We now know, from the notes in Field's journal, that as Peter was dying, he said to him, 'I hated you all along.' He taunted him too, reminding him that he had changed his will and, as a result, 'this is my house'. If we are to believe that this entry is genuine, in the sense that this is truly how Field behaved as Peter lay dying, rather than simply something he later invented for effect, the last words that Peter heard were not of love and thanks, but of hatred and vitriol. It also suggests gerontophobia, rather than a sexual desire for his elderly partner.

I wanted to discover more about the first coroner's inquiry and why it had concluded that Peter had died accidentally as a result of acute alcohol intoxication. It reminded me of the death of Nancy Emms, raped and strangled by Kenneth Erskine, and the assumption she had died of 'natural causes', which her doctor duly recorded on her death certificate, and, of course, all the murders committed by Shipman. As a GP he could easily gain ready and legal access to drugs and complete his own paperwork about his patients' sudden and untimely deaths, but why had the coroner been so certain that Peter had died of acute alcohol poisoning?

If you want to see a copy of a pathologist report after a post-mortem in the UK, you can request this from the coroner's office in exchange for a small fee. The Coroners Act of 1962 makes provision in law for an inquest into a death and all depositions, post-mortem reports and verdict records collected to be preserved by the coroner and made available to the public. So I duly paid the £27 required and asked to see a copy of Peter's full post-mortem report. I wondered on what basis the conclusion had been reached and who might have given evidence. Were some of the doctors who Peter had seen at the practice in Buckingham called to give evidence? Was Field himself called as a witness and, if so, what did he say? It seemed like a pretty straightforward administrative process to obtain the report and answer these questions, and the official I initially spoke to about the request was helpful. In the end, however, I would be disappointed.

After waiting several months, partly as a result of COVID-19, which meant that the new senior coroner Crispin Butler was rarely in the office, I eventually received a reply in August 2020 turning down my request to see the full report. I was advised by email that Mr Butler did not believe that it was 'appropriate for a copy of the post-mortem report to be released given the intervening events and investigation and the distress that this might cause to Peter's family', and nor was I seemingly a 'proper person' to have possession of it.

This seemed to me to be a very self-serving position to have adopted.

After all, it was precisely because of 'intervening events' and the new police investigation which had led to Field's arrest that I wanted to see a copy of the full report. I wanted to assess how the original inquiry had got things so woefully wrong, by coming to the conclusion that Peter had died accidentally when he had actually been poisoned. And surely it was that mistake, rather than my asking how that mistake had been made, which had caused the distress to Peter's family? Denying me an opportunity to scrutinise their processes and procedures also allowed the coroner's office to helpfully maintain their public appearance of infallibility, even though they clearly messed up in this case. Finally, it's also hard to ignore the secrecy surrounding all of this, and therefore who it is that actually has the right to information in our culture. I have always taken the view that if information is collected about people, then it is the people who have a right to know what that information is.

Mr Butler's email ended by promising me the return of my £27.

I'm still waiting.

Field would have almost certainly got away with Peter's murder if he hadn't then decided to move on to Ann Moore-Martin. As Ann's health declined, her family became suspicious and took their suspicions to the police. It was just as well they did. This would set in motion a chain of events that now means we know exactly what did happen to Peter.

But all of that was in the future, and back in the winter of 2015 there was a funeral to organise at Stowe Parish Church.

Perhaps funerals accomplish more for the living than they do for the dead, but they can also sometimes help to restore dignity to the person who has died, especially if the process of their dying had been undignified. There would be some friends in attendance who would recall their final unsettling encounters with Peter in the preceding months, when he had not been himself and therefore the funeral would at least allow them to remember him as he once was, as opposed to the person he had become. So while more generally as a culture we may be in the process of dispensing with organised religion, Christianity still provides for many a comfort and consolation in its ancient rituals for managing the dead, and helping people to grieve – to find the right words to say to remember, and to celebrate as much as mourn.

At Peter's service, Field delivered the eulogy and said that the congregation in the church was 'the legacy he meant to leave'. He went on to describe Peter as an 'ardent believer, father to the needy, reader, author, teacher, preacher, master of his field and craft'. I was later struck by that phrase – 'master of his field'. It seemed to me that Field was almost certainly playing games, as Peter was not the 'master' of Field. Field then reminded the congregation of a night the previous November, when Peter was 'gleeful, sparkler in his hand, writing his name in the air amongst shrieks of laughter'. It was an attractive, cheerful image that must have brought a smile to the faces of many in the church and, for some, peace and solace. However, it was also a manipulation; a carefully constructed deceit and linguistic misdirection; it was part of a self-serving narrative constructed by an unreliable narrator. The congregation didn't know at that point that this image of a happier time was conjured up by the man who had murdered Peter by repeatedly poisoning him, and who, as a result, was also about to come into a lot of money.

In July 2016, Field inherited £20,000 in Peter's will and then, when the house in Maids Moreton was sold in December

2016, he also received half of the profit, which amounted to £142,000. A fall in house prices meant that this was slightly less than the £160,000 that had been envisaged at one stage. In June 2020, Oxford Crown Court ordered Field to repay £146,561, after confiscation proceedings were brought against him under the Proceeds of Crime Act.

*

As I continued to research the case, a nagging question hung over me. Did Peter have any idea of Field's true nature? I wondered if during the five years of their relationship, he had ever seen through Field's play-acting, caught him dressing up in front of the mirror, mimicking voices and shucking off his own identity to become someone else. Had he ever caught Field, like Dickie had caught Tom Ripley? I believe Peter did.

Earlier, I reproduced some of Peter's correspondence with Dr Pryce, about how he was experiencing hallucinations, and feeling like he was losing his mind. I was intrigued by a number of interesting possibilities which are revealed in the text.

Why, for example, did Peter feel the need to mention Field and Martyn Smith at all? They are hardly relevant to the story that he is outlining to his GP, but Peter clearly wanted them named. Perhaps it was merely gratitude, or perhaps he was naming the perpetrators and, powerless to act himself, was crying out for help. I also find it difficult to ignore Peter's use of 'illusion' rather than hallucination. Illusion means trickery and deception – or magic perpetrated by someone whose stock in trade was to make things disappear and reappear through misdirection and sleight of hand. Words were important to Peter. It is possible that he was trying to draw attention to the real source of his medical problems, which could be terrifying and confusing one day, only to magically disappear the next, before the illness suddenly struck again.

There was certainly an edge to Field that Peter didn't like. For example, at Christmas 2012, just after Field had started his MA and Peter's *A Bitter Heart* was published, Field gave Peter six poems called 'Truest Jest', which were written about Peter. It was a present that hinted at what their relationship had been like in the previous months, although Field would later claim that the poems were simply preparation for 'rap battles'. These poems were hurtful and abusive, with Field repeatedly calling Peter a 'fag', and included lines such as 'There's nothing in your future when I do you'; 'the hospitality I'll give him's a hospital visit'; and 'I run in to save like a paramedic, to lift him up from his flaws like a [S]tannah stairlift.' Another verse in the same poem read:

> He's demanding and he's maddening,
> And he thinks that I am mad at him.
> I'm asking *isn't it fanciful to act as if*
> *I'm angry just because I'm masculine?*

Field would later claim that this was all just meant as a joke, that it was a 'jest', but Peter didn't see the funny side. He returned the Christmas present in kind, writing his own poem, which he called 'Ben':

> Consider now an obscure youth called Ben,
> Caustic pedant, laughably vain,
> Recently bearded with searing black eyes,

Aspiring to become one of the tough guys.
For Irish Muldoon he hopelessly pleads,
A nonentity whom nobody reads.
Deceptive and disloyal as a friend,
Ben uses people for unworthy ends.
Willing to wound and happy to strike,
Returning kindness with sneering dislike.
Described himself as a conceited teen,
A serious <u>man</u> he has never been.
Hurting others is his special pleasure,
Cruel disregard a happy leisure.
Skinhead with pseudo-intellectual specs,
Befriend him and he your reputation wrecks.
Witness: in eighteen lines more has been said,
Than in the mass scribblings from Ben's poisoned head.

There's a lot going on in this poem.

Peter describes Field as obscure, caustic, vain, deceptive and disloyal and takes a swipe at the subject of his MA dissertation, the contemporary Irish poet Paul Muldoon. The 'nobody reads' phrase, rather than being a criticism of Muldoon, is perhaps meant to contrast with the poets that Peter loves and had taught and written about. More than this, he describes Field as someone who uses people and who would be happy to 'wound' and 'strike', as 'hurting others is his special pleasure'. This latter phrase hints at the sadism of the cutting penknives, the drugging and the gaslighting which is to come, and the psychopathic nature of Field. Peter's underlining of the noun 'man', followed by the words 'he has never been', would seem to be a riposte to Field's description of himself as 'masculine'.

Peter is deliberately mocking Field's aspiring 'tough guy' persona, and 'recently bearded' image. We can also read the phrase 'recently bearded' as gay slang for trying to hide his true sexual orientation.

Finally, it is clear that Peter worries that his friendship with Field had wrecked his reputation, although of course he would eventually go through with a betrothal ceremony and later change his will. Even so, this poem indicates that Peter knew what Field was capable of doing; before Field started to drug him and make him dependent, he could see through the new, carefully constructed image that was being built before his eyes, and glimpse the cruel, sneering, sadistic reality of the 'poisoned head' behind the 'pseudo-intellectual specs'.

Perhaps more than anything else, what 'Truest Jest' and 'Ben' reveal is just how literary and bookish Peter and Field were, to the extent that they even argue in rhyme. In one sense they followed a literary, Romantic tradition of sending poems to each other, as Coleridge and Wordsworth had done. The written word is clearly important to them in all kinds of different ways, but especially as a means to express their emotions: their words convey both love and anger; attraction and repulsion; joy and hatred. Words were who they were, and their words therefore tell us a story. Harnessed in the right way, these words also offer to us a way of understanding and can guide us through the most complex of their behaviours. The plot of Peter's last novel in particular, with all its strange twists and turns, offers a valuable insight into their relationship, and holds alarming similarities to the real-life events that took place in Maids Moreton.

'Plot', of course, has two different meanings. It can mean

a secretly made plan, or we use it to describe a sequence of events in a film, play or story. And, in the same way that I wondered whether Peter was communicating with his GP about the plot unfolding about his health, to what extent was the plot of *A Bitter Heart* the literary template for how Field would come to commit murder? A close reading of the novel suggests that Field used the book as a literary weapon, stealing the plot as his ultimate act of disloyalty and vengeance to kill Peter.

*

A Bitter Heart was the last book that Peter wrote, although it was published in September 2012, three years before *A Wide Wide Sea*. It is much shorter than his other two books, consisting of only fifteen chapters and is under 180 pages in length, and would be better described as a novella rather than a novel. It is dedicated to one of his former colleagues at Stowe School but there is a 'special thanks' to Field for his 'proof reading and necessary emendations'. I would later organise to meet up with my old university friend Professor Philip Horne, now Professor of English at University College London and an expert on Henry James – seemingly Peter's favourite novelist – and I also took the opportunity to ask him about this phrase rather than just quiz him about James. Philip thought that it 'sounds like a private message – are there perhaps sex scenes in what he writes? "Emendations" is about style and when there's something wrong in the text; something that doesn't make sense. So it is about substituting something which is correct, for something that the author has written incorrectly.'

Early in my research, I had decided to write to Field, having located the prison that he'd been sent to after his conviction.

In the second of the two letters I sent, I asked what these 'necessary emendations' might have been; his failure to reply means that I can only guess. However, Field was clearly central to the completion of *A Bitter Heart* – an issue I discuss below. Let's first study the novella from the 'orthodox approach' that Peter would employ when discussing a book at the Stowe Reading Group, by considering the plotting of the narrative; central themes; language; characterisation; and, finally, 'the point of it all'.

The novella is set in Manchester, where of course Peter had once taught, and the narrative follows the fates of two university students, Kate Brathwaite and Rob Hadfield, boyfriend and girlfriend, although their respective friends also make an appearance, including Rob's best friend Christopher Wood – 'Woody' – whom we are told 'had attended a Buckinghamshire grammar school'.

Philip Horne's question as to whether there were sex scenes in the novel made me reconsider Rob's surname in a somewhat different light. He was Robert 'Rob' Hadfield. The shortening of 'Robert' to 'Rob' is straightforward enough, and of course mirrors how 'Benjamin' invariably becomes 'Ben', but there is also a teasing pun in the fact that Rob's surname is 'Had–Field'. Had Peter 'had' Field?

The other two main characters are Brian Hadfield, Rob's father, a widower who 'shuts up like a clam the moment it [the death of his wife] is mentioned', and Mara Braithwaite, who is Kate's mother and also a widow. Mara is described as being 'quietly courageous', 'imaginative' and 'always immaculately presented'. It is through Mara's eyes that we are offered a description of Rob: 'what a handsome boy he is, she thought, with his dark hair and eyes and his finely sculpted cheek-bones, his jaw defined by unshaven fleece', and we are told that he has a 'lean, athletic frame'. We are also introduced to Mara's in-laws, Jane and Norman, who are members of the United Reformed Church, rather than the Church of England. This allows Peter to discuss matters of faith, although perhaps more significantly, it was the United Reformed Church that, in 2012, voted to allow the blessing of same-sex civil partner-ships, and in 2016 to allow its churches to conduct same-sex marriages.

The novella is punctuated with a number of themes that preoccupied Peter throughout his literary career, especially in relation to sexuality and faith.

Kate, who is studying psychology, is still a virgin. 'She did not feel ready,' it is explained, 'for intercourse quite yet. She had no moral objections but she had not had a regular boyfriend before'. It is implied that this put a strain on her relationship with Rob. That Kate had no 'moral objections' to sex is a development within Peter's writing, no doubt mirror-ing changes in his own life, or at least in his thinking. Kate is also increasingly annoying Rob: she's whiny and irritating, and seems incapable of having a proper relationship. She even makes a pass at Woody.

In an obvious nod to George Eliot's *The Mill on the Floss*, the novella opens with Kate having been knocked, or pushed, into the river by Rob:

She was instantly aware of the water's overpowering, icy energy ... The shock of colliding with this unfamiliar, hostile medium rapidly gave way to the panic of absolute terror. She could not swim. The current swept her along. It was not just that she was sinking. It was as though some malignantly destructive force of immense power was violently pulling her under. She screamed, horribly aware of her impending doom, but the sound seemed to tinkle hopelessly in space, her head bobbing above the immense, empty surface of the river as it drove relentlessly and dispassionately onwards.

This is some of Peter's best writing and consciously uses Romantic themes to create a sense of danger, awe and horror. The river, in itself always a useful literary metaphor, and one especially used by Wordsworth, is an 'unfamiliar, hostile medium' that sweeps Kate along, so that she is unable to resist what is happening to her; her screams 'tinkle hopelessly'. What's worse is that it's not just the current that is sweeping Kate to her death, but also some 'malignantly destructive force of immense power' which was pulling her under. Ironically, contemporary movies, especially those within the horror genre, will often 'punish' women who are sexually active, but here a woman seems to be being punished for being sexually inexperienced.

This dramatic and deadly opening, which echoes a similar deadly and dramatic opening in *Between Boy and Man*, sets up the narrative and the moral questions at the heart of the story. It's an incident, we are told, that 'is the sort of thing that happens in the news – to other people'. Rob had been running on the path beside the river as Kate had been walking along, and they had collided. Did Rob bump into Kate accidentally, a collision that resulted in her falling in the river, causing her death, or did he deliberately push her? He had jumped into the river to try to save Kate, but he had apparently been unable to do so. We therefore also have to decide if Rob had been heroic in his actions, or quite deliberately homicidal.

At the start of the novella Mara, Kate's mother, has made up her own mind and has settled on an explanation. Over a cup of tea with Rob, she tells him, 'No! No! Rob, you did everything you could. You know I think that. You risked your own life. The policeman said that you were heroic.' This establishes the idea of blame and forgiveness, and whether Rob can ever forgive himself. As he is about to leave, Mara suggests to Rob, 'Perhaps I could share you with your father? Treat you as my son?' Rob thinks that she could indeed become his 'surrogate mother'. When he leaves, they embrace: 'he was clean and fresh and firm, light but strong; his body was faintly scented with a subtly dry deodorant. She was sorry to see him leave.'

However, their burgeoning relationship becomes more problematic, and thereafter impossible, when in a poorly worked plot twist Mara decides that Rob did in fact murder Kate after all, and so she sets out to 'destroy that diabolical boy'. 'It's murder,' she tells Rob when she confronts him, 'that's what it is. You murdered her. Oh, my God.' Mara knew that this would be difficult, but

The police must be told. The boy had lied to them. Or, at the very least, he had withheld vital information, germane to the truth, the even more hideous truth, at the centre of that trivial encounter. The problem was, she realised early on, that he would lie to them again ... criminals got away with anything these days, murder included. You only need to read the newspapers or switch on the television news to understand that.

Unsurprisingly, Mara finds this distressing, but has no solace in her religious in-laws and their faith. She doesn't want to forgive Rob. She is not sleeping properly, 'sleeping so badly, with chimeras of horror stalking the darkness' that she visits her GP, Dr Barrington, to ask for medication. She is prescribed flurazepam and, when the first course of treatment has been completed, she returns to the doctor to get some more. Dr Barrington asks,

> Flurazepam again? And shall we stick with the stronger 30mg version? It's not as though you are the kind of patient who is likely to misuse them.

When she takes the tablets, Mara becomes 'groggy', and has 'difficulty in achieving any sort of coherence'. Even so, she hatches a plan to get even with Rob while tending Kate's grave. 'The plan was simple really. She would add more sugar than usual to Rob's tea and add two or three crushed flurazepam tablets to the cup ... when he fell into a deep sleep, she would kill him.' Events don't work out this way, and we next find Mara at the place where Kate had fallen into the river, where she is going to commit suicide:

> She opened the packet of flurazepam, took three tablets from the foil which encased them and put them inside her mouth. Then she unscrewed the bottle of vodka and took a large swig to wash the sleeping pills down. She had never drunk vodka before ... Mara repeated this process several times until there were no tablets left. Her stomach retched; she felt sick; she fell backwards against the osier bush;

her head was swimming. She embraced the accelerating descent into unconsciousness with relief.

Rob, making his own way along the path, discovers Mara and calls an ambulance: 'What have you done? Don't say that you've drunk all this vodka. What was in the packet? Oh my God!' Too much alcohol and an overdose of flurazepam. As he finishes his call to the emergency services, Mara regains a little consciousness and opens her eyes. Rob is holding Mara in his arms, but he realises she is looking at him with 'unforgiving hatred'. Indeed, Mara tells him bluntly, 'I hate you', to which Rob replies,

> I am so sorry about what happened here. I didn't push Kate. Honestly, I didn't. I wouldn't ever have done such a terrible thing. I'm not like that. You've got to believe me! Please! It was an accident – a terrible accident.

Mara simply shakes her head. She cannot forgive Rob. Then she dies.

The novella ends with two different scenes of reflection. In the first, Rob has lunch with his father and, in the second, which closes the story, we join Mara's in-laws celebrating their silver wedding anniversary. Jane's concluding reflection is that 'God has been good to us both'. Over the lunch between father and son, Rob laments that Mara wouldn't believe what happened to Kate had been a dreadful accident, and that 'she actually thinks – thought – that I had deliberately pushed Kate into the water'. Brian reassures his son:

Well it should go without saying that nobody else will have thought that. Anyone who knows you at all would realise the absurdity of the accusation.

*

Finally, echoing how Peter would analyse a book at the SRG, what is 'the point of it all'? *A Bitter Heart* would, on the surface, appear to be about the need for forgiveness: of living your life positively, rather than allowing hatred, resentment and bitterness to determine the pattern of your existence as a human being. The ending of the novella at Jane and Norman's silver wedding anniversary party, and Jane's observation that 'God has been good to us both', returns us once again to the centrality of faith in Peter's writing. However, as I have mentioned, the fact that Jane and Norman are members of the United Reformed Church suggests how Peter's attitudes about his sexuality and reconciling it with his faith were beginning to change, even if the novella itself is avowedly heterosexual.

Above all else, it is sex rather than sexuality which seems to be important, and throughout the narrative we never lose sight of the significance of this within the plot, or how it will impact the lives of the characters. This takes a variety of forms: Kate is a virgin and her virginity is offered as an explanation for the increasing tension in her relationship with Rob; Mara, at least at the start, seems to sexually fantasise about Rob, who himself will go on to have a relationship while studying abroad (and there is therefore a textual echo here of Peter's coming-of-age novel *A Wide Wide Sea*); and Jane and Norman have, of course, been happily married for twenty-five years.

Nor should we ignore the powerful metaphor that Peter

introduces at the start of the novella – 'the unfamiliar hostile medium'. In other words, the river that consumes Kate, with the implication that this unfamiliar hostile medium is about sexual feelings. If this is so, why is it 'a malignantly destructive force of immense power' that violently pulls her under, and why would this eventually be the same spot where Mara would commit suicide, dying in Rob's arms? It is tempting to conclude that it is the author himself who is coming to terms not only with his own sexual identity but also his own sexual experience.

In looking at the point of the novella more critically, a good place to start is to question why both Kate and Mara need to die. Let me put this as a series of questions. Does Kate die because she is sexually inexperienced and doesn't seem able to establish a proper relationship? Is it her virginity which we are being asked to judge as problematic? And, as far as her mother is concerned, does Mara have to die not only because this allows us to realise that having a bitter heart is no way to live, but also because she had once harboured uncertain sexual feelings for Rob? Mara has nowhere to go within the narrative, no moral or practical means of reconciling what has happened and what she feels. What is beyond doubt is that both characters had unresolved sexual longings for the 'diabolical boy', although neither had been able to consummate that relationship before they perished.

In *Between Boy and Man*, I suggested that Peter was both Alexander Scott, the Head of English at Moreton College and the Reverend John Donaldson, and that this 'splitting' allowed him to discuss both his love of literature and deal with matters of faith and sexuality. *A Bitter Heart* feels more mature thematically than *Between Boy and Man*, partly due to the change in setting and the ages of the main characters, although it is still possible to discern Peter in a number of the characters and their dilemmas. Is he not Kate, who had never had a regular partner before? Like Kate he doesn't seem to be able to have a 'proper grown up' relationship. He's Mara too, who fantasises about Rob and offers to us various descriptions about how he looks and smells. We can also see Peter in Brian, calmly reassuring his son that no one could possibly believe that he was capable of committing murder.

Of course, we are no further forward in truly understanding if Peter had in fact 'had' Field, although as we know that words are important to them both, the temptation must be to suggest that he had. That's more mature too.

And what of Field's 'necessary emendations'? Was offering the surname for Rob's character one of those emendations, or are there other textual clues about what the emendations might have been? Can we detect 'Woody', for example, in some of Field's classmates at university, who he described as 'boring'? 'Woody' is often an insult used for people who are thought of as being stupid, and we know that Field liked to think of himself as an intellectual cut above his peers.

It is also slang for an erect penis.

However, perhaps the most obvious places to look for emendations are in the mentions of flurazepam, including the appropriate dosage that would be prescribed.

Poor, trusting, fictional Dr Barrington – and we know from Peter's journal that on the morning he started his part-time job at UB he had an appointment at the Swan Practice with the very real Dr Roger Harrington. The fictional doctor happily dispenses the drugs that Mara would ultimately wash down with vodka to commit suicide. This raises another 'point of it all'. If my reading is correct, just how much of *A Bitter Heart* was a prophetic prototype for Field's murder of Peter, who, we should not forget, was originally believed to have died of acute alcohol poisoning?

*

It is impossible to read *A Bitter Heart* without noticing the connections to Peter's death. Indeed, I would go as far as to suggest that these connections are so overwhelming they were a template Field used. I wonder to what extent Peter was conscious of how the plot of his novella was providing a blueprint for his own murder, or whether he was so blinded by his love for Field that he couldn't see his own story becoming reality. The 'chimeras of horror stalking the darkness' and Mara's 'groggy ... disorientating wilderness' where she had 'difficulty in achieving any sort of coherence' clearly mirrors what Peter would later describe of his own condition when he wrote to Dr Pryce, and of being unable to remember names, dates and places, speaking in German and having 'illusions'. It was that 'disorientating wilderness' and lack of coherence that people noticed at Peter's book launch.

Nor did Mara, or Peter, feel that there would be any point in contacting the police, as the 'diabolical boy' would merely lie again. Even so, this has always been something which perplexed me about the case. Why did Peter, who clearly understood a great deal about Field's personality and could even have harboured suspicions about the true source of his illness, not simply call the police? Perhaps this behaviour was merely a manifestation of the domestic violence that patterned their relationship, and so he felt that he had no one to turn to.

Whatever the reason, Field was able to get away with murder because no one alerted the authorities to his activities (which Field would call 'manoeuvres' in his journals). Peter, therefore, is like Mara dying in Rob's arms, but that 'extraordinary intimacy' he experienced with Field merely revealed a hateful 'concentrated enmity'.

Having at last found love, I get the sense that Peter just couldn't bear to let it go, even if it was a love(r) that was literally killing him. If he had some inkling about Field, he didn't want to call the police, or report him to the authorities. To do so would be to acknowledge that he had acted foolishly – like Kate making a pass at Woody. It might have been penknives that they had exchanged during their betrothal ceremony but, as far as Peter was concerned, they denoted unending love, like traditional wedding rings. So he'd made his bed, and now he was going to die on it.

However, read in this way *A Bitter Heart* acts like a *memento mori*: a literary reminder that we all have to die. Sadly, I get the sense that, in the end, Peter no longer had the strength, nor perhaps the will, to resist Field's final, deadly manoeuvres. He was not so much going gently into that good night as succumbing to a malevolent force that was pulling him down and taking him there.

*

The most obvious link between the novella and what happens to Peter is of course the alcohol and the use of flurazepam. First, it was going to be used by Mara to kill Rob, at least within the tentative plot that she hatched. She was going to surreptitiously crush the drugs into his tea and then kill him, after he had fallen into a deep sleep. Second, when

144

Mara swallows the pills herself, she washes them down with alcohol. Of course, it is vodka in the novella and whisky in real life, but the connections are clear, even down to the fact that it would be Rob, just like Field, who calls the emergency services asking for help. Did perhaps fictional Dr Barrington's trusting observation that Mara wasn't 'the type of patient who is likely to misuse them' also echo real-life conversations with Dr Harrington?

Perhaps the greatest link is not only the fact that Kate dies, but also that Rob is reassured by his father that anyone who thinks that her death was a murder would realise that they were making 'an absurd accusation'. He just isn't the type of young man who could commit a murder; he's a handsome university student getting on with his studies. Anyone could see that! Mara initially thought of him as having been 'heroic', which mirrored Peter's first flush of boundless enthusiasm about Field, and of course we don't like to be disappointed by our heroes. Even so, we only have Rob's assurance that the collision was indeed an accident, and Mara's fear that 'criminals get away with anything these days, murder included' exactly echoes the immediate aftermath of Peter's death. Who had suggested that line? Was it also a necessary emendation? No one thought that Peter's death could have been murder either, and there were even some who believed that Field had been, if not quite heroic, at least stalwart in the care and attention he had given to Peter. In the same way that Mara is presented as increasingly disturbed, so too would Peter be described by Field as suffering from dementia, and simply drinking too much.

Finally, what kills Kate is not just the river itself, but also a 'malignantly destructive force of immense power' that pulls her under. 'Malignant' can mean malicious, spiteful and vindictive, and a 'malignantly destructive force' conjures up a sense of overpowering evil. In *A Bitter Heart*, this force is what is sometimes called 'natural evil' – it is the force of the current of the river. However, as far as Peter's murder is concerned, we have a different form of evil: the moral evil of Ben Field; he really is a 'diabolical boy' and I believe that Peter knew that only too well.

Did Field think that anyone who called Peter's death 'murder' would be seen as making 'an absurd accusation'? Perhaps. When he was first arrested with Martyn Smith in March 2017, their conversations were secretly recorded by the police as they sat in the back of a police van. In the recording Field can be heard telling Smith that he 'expected to get away with most of it'.

He very nearly did.

It was here that I realised that, throughout my research, Field had been a dark shadow hanging over me. He was like a bad smell in the kitchen that, for a few days, you think you can live with, but then it becomes so noxious and overwhelming you really do have to do something about it: clean the work surfaces, throw out any rotten vegetables, move the fridge – has something died behind there? You know that eventually you are going to have to take a look.

It was time to think a little more clearly about Benjamin Luke Field.

CHAPTER SEVEN

Benjamin Field

'It gives a fascinating insight into the work of
Paul Muldoon and the mind of the author'

Five-star review by IAN FIELD of
*For 'Work' Read 'Work': Reading Ergodics
and Ergodic Reading in Paul Muldoon*
by Ben Field, Amazon, 27 November 2014

Sometimes there are advantages that come from having worked in HM Prison Service and having friends who still do. As I've mentioned, at the very start of my research I found out the prison where Field was located and sent him a letter at HMP Bullingdon in Bicester, asking if he would be willing to speak with me. I wasn't certain if he would reply, although I did wonder if his narcissism would get the better of him, and that we'd start a correspondence. That's happened before. In my office at home I have a lever-arch file filled with correspondence sent to me by the Scottish serial killer and necrophile Dennis Nilsen, who liked to talk endlessly about the murders he committed, and I regularly receive unsolicited letters from murderers who are serving their sentences and who have tracked down my university address. However, Field never did respond to that first letter, or to a follow-up that I sent to him when he was moved to HMP Durham.

One of my friends from my prison days, who works as a forensic psychologist, wasn't in the least surprised: 'The whole basis of his offending has been about control. He likes being in control and there's no payoff for him through writing to you.' When I suggested that Field seemed to me to be narcissistic, my friend agreed, but thought that his desire to control would outweigh all other considerations and so that would be the basis on whether or not he would write back: 'He's trying to control the process of your writing, and also what it is that you eventually write. In that way, as you know, he's trying to control you.'

This seemed to me like a good assessment. Over the years I've got used to having to explain to students that it really is only on TV and in the movies that violent offenders want to spill the beans and tell detectives all about the crimes they've committed, and why they did it. In my experience, murderers, and especially serial murderers, are usually silent and uncommunicative; silence is a readily used means of trying to control the narrative. 'No comment.' In fact, it is the only tactic that they have left. That's why I suspect both Fred West and Harold Shipman committed suicide – death is the ultimate form of silence; of 'no comment' – and they refused when they were alive to ever speak about the murders that they had committed.

However, this wasn't quite true of Field more generally. It

seemed to me that he had been very talkative: his voice had often been heard in the town, at the university and in church. He'd left emails and notes about what he had been doing and thinking; he'd written a thesis that the university had published. As I have mentioned, after the deaths of Peter and of Ann Moore-Martin he'd even preached a sermon on the theme of 'Thou Shalt Not Kill' at his father's church, a recording of which was on the church's website for a time. Also, rather memorably, Field took to the witness stand during his trial, to give evidence in his own defence. That's very unusual for someone charged with murder and, in Field's case, merely served to demonstrate to the court his rampant narcissism. After his conviction the press would come to describe him as 'evil', 'twisted' and, focusing on the more lurid sexual aspects of his behaviour, as a 'toy boy' who had had multiple sexual partners of both genders.

All in all, I'd actually heard a great deal about Field's thoughts and opinions about himself and of other people. He might be silent and uncommunicative now, but that wasn't always the case.

I'd also listened to what his former friends had said about him when they had been at school together, and heard what some of his former girlfriends remembered of him. I'd also interviewed a number of people who knew him in other contexts. In fact, I felt that I knew a great deal about Field and that left me with a problem: if he replied to my letters, and perhaps sent me a visiting order to come to the prison, how would I go about managing my interactions with him?

While I was working directly with offenders in a penal setting, I'd been trained to administer something called a

P-SCAN. Over time, I would run hundreds of these P-SCANS, which allowed me to draw some conclusions about an offender, someone suspected of having committed a crime, or other people of interest who I might have to interview. The 'P' stands for psychopathy. The P-SCAN is *not* a clinical diagnosis, but rather an 'early warning system': a screening device that can provide you with clues, perhaps even a working hypothesis, about the nature of the person with whom you might have to work. So a high score on the P-SCAN would perhaps make me want to adopt or change a particular interviewing strategy, given that such a score would suggest that my interviewee was most likely going to play 'head games', and to try to manipulate or con me. A high P-SCAN score *suggests* psychopathy.

The great advantage of the P-SCAN is that it can be completed without the individual being present, on the basis of information that has already been collected about that person in the form of police, probation or court reports; interviews that have been conducted with family members, or friends; knowledge of that individual's previous offending history; what he had been like at school; the pattern of his employment; or even newspaper accounts, should his case have attracted media attention, and which invariably throws other types of information into the mix.

The P-SCAN consists of ninety items depicting quite specific behaviours which represent the three key facets of psychopathy: *interpersonal* (his relationships with others, such as being glib; grandiose; lying; manipulative); *affective* (this facet is about the individual's feelings and emotions, such as having a lack of empathy, remorse or guilt); and *lifestyle* (such as having a need for stimulation, being impulsive, or having a parasitic lifestyle involving many people, and so forth). Each of the items is rated on a three-point scale. So scoring 0 for an item means that it does not apply to the individual, while 1 indicates that it applies to a certain extent and, finally, 2 would be given as a score when it is clear that this item is characteristic of the individual. Scores are calculated for each of the three facets, added together and then divided by three to give a P-SCAN 'Total Score'. This Total Score indicates the level of concern you should have when interviewing such an individual: someone who scores less than 10 would be of 'very low concern', whereas someone who scores 30 and above would be of 'serious concern'. Scoring at this level would, according to the guidance, suggest that:

The person of interest may have many or most of the features that define psychopathy. Such a person is likely to be egocentric, callous, cold-blooded, predatory, impulsive, irresponsible, dominant, deceptive, manipulative, and lacking in empathy, guilt, or genuine remorse for socially deviant and criminal acts. People of this sort do not share the attitudes, thoughts, and feelings that motivate and guide the behaviours of most people. Their main concerns are for themselves and for exerting power and control over others. They are quite capable of intimidation and violence to attain their needs and wants, but their actions are 'a matter of process,' without the emotional colouring that characterizes the violent acts of others.

I thought that it would be helpful to administer a P-SCAN on Field, but while I was in the process of doing so his MA dissertation popped through my letterbox – I'd ordered it from Amazon and, before long, I became totally engrossed in the task of reading it. It was an extraordinary and, I felt, very revealing document.

The P-SCAN would have to wait.

*

In my academic career I have read thousands of masters dissertations and supervised hundreds of masters students. I can honestly say that I've encountered some excellent dissertations, as well as a few that were, to put it politely, rubbish. However, I have never read a dissertation at the masters level that I thought should be published, although perhaps this merely reveals a difference between teaching criminology and teaching English literature. Even at the next level, only two of the twenty doctoral dissertations that I have supervised were published directly as monographs. In fact I used to joke, partly to help ease the feelings of desperation that some postgraduate students develop, that they shouldn't worry unduly about what they had written as very few people would actually read their work – perhaps just me as their supervisor, the external examiner and their parents.

I was therefore more than a little surprised to discover that Field's masters dissertation had been published by the University of Buckingham Press, the small publishing arm of the university that had been founded in 2005, although a majority of its shares have apparently now been acquired by Legend Times. It seemed to me like a very public endorsement of his work, of him as a student at the university, and also implied that UB was investing in him as a scholar for the future. On the book's back cover Professor John Drew of UB described the work as 'a tour de force' and 'in the idiosyncratic manner of its subject'; Tim Kendall, who is a poet as well as Professor of English at the University of Exeter, thought it 'extremely impressive ... brilliant frivolity'. 'Frivolity' makes the book sound enticing, but just so that you are a little less tempted, the title of Field's work is *For 'Work' Read 'Work': Reading Ergodics and Ergodic Reading in Paul Muldoon*. Even if you had heard of the Irish poet Paul Muldoon, which I confess I had not at that stage, you would also have to be aware, if only in passing, with what 'ergodic literature', or more generally 'ergodicity', actually is and, again, I plead ignorance. I am in no place to judge the quality of Field's dissertation and therefore how suitable it was to be published, but I have to admit that even with my superficial knowledge of this field I was, well, staggered.

I wonder to what extent Kendall's 'frivolity' and Drew's 'idiosyncratic manner' are meant as clues that the commendations are not what they first appear to be.

Let's leave to one side for the moment what this endorsement of Field's work implies more broadly, or even what he writes about, and simply review his acknowledgements. The book was published in November 2014 and so I thought that it might have been dedicated to Peter Farquhar, with whom he was now living – and, of course, the pair had gone through a betrothal ceremony just six months prior. I was mistaken; Peter is not mentioned at all. Peter would seem to have already outlived his usefulness. Field was possibly experiencing 'buyer's remorse' and already planning to move on to someone else. Perhaps he already had, but in any event poor Peter would be dead in under a year. In the acknowledgements Field does thank Professor Stefan Hawlin, his supervisor, who 'graciously suffered during the creation of this work', and Professor Tim Kendall, who had examined an 'early version of this work'.

I emailed Professor Hawlin at UB, explaining that I wanted to discuss the dissertation, but he replied saying that 'issues of confidentiality' about former students prevented him from doing so. His refusal neatly echoed the reaction of the Coroner's Office to my request to see the full post-mortem report. I clearly wasn't a 'proper person' for UB either. His reply also seemed disingenuous, for I did not want to discuss Field as a former student – I wanted to know about what he had written and why the university had chosen to publish it.

I also emailed Professor Kendall at Exeter University and he was kind enough to get back to me more substantively. At first he thought I had contacted the wrong Tim Kendall and sent by return the email address for the National Clinical Director for Mental Health NHS England. I had to reply with a little more detail: 'I am sorry if I have made a mistake, but are you not Professor of Poetry at Exeter and who has written about Paul Muldoon. Field's dissertation was about Muldoon and a "Professor Tim Kendall" is referenced within the bibliography twice and quoted on the back cover. Is that not you?' This time Tim took a little longer to respond, as he was going back over his old emails and notes to see if he had indeed examined someone at UB called Ben Field. This time, when he replied, Tim said, 'Well this was all new to me – or so it seemed.' He continued:

I did write a report for U of Buckingham seven years ago, relating to a candidate called Ben Field. I have no recollection of the work, and I didn't meet the candidate or visit the university. It was an MA by Res[earch] and it was online.

Tim then explained that he had been external examiner and that Professor John Drew, who he had also never met, was the internal examiner. He added: 'Unless my memory is playing tricks on me I haven't read a subsequent monograph.' This implies that he never gave permission for his comments on the 'early version' of the dissertation to be used as an endorsement on the published monograph. In response to this earlier version, he stated that the dissertation was good enough to pass and might form the basis of a PhD, or even a scholarly monograph in the future, but that 'it would need some serious editing'. As for the 'brilliant frivolity' line, Tim explains that his comment alludes to the fact that Field had outlined how he could play games with his dissertation but, of course, he also 'wanted the examiners to award a mark: on what basis? It is after all our prerogative to find these games unnecessary, inappropriate, unenlightening, [and] frivolous.' He also said that by page 40 of the dissertation Field had still only used one of Muldoon's poems.

There were further surprises in the acknowledgements. Field 'most importantly' wants to thank his family: 'My earnest appreciation for the tolerance of my family, not only during this writing but across the period of time between my birth and now. It has been noted.' This seems to hint at something much deeper than those 'grateful thanks' one normally encounters, and it was impossible to ignore that in his father's five-star Amazon review he thought that the dissertation allowed him an insight not only into Muldoon's work, but also into the 'mind of the author'. Amazon hardly seems to be the proper place for a father to be discussing his son's book, let alone his 'mind'. Worse was to come. Field ends his acknowledgements: 'Finally, a special mention to my brother Tom Field. Chapter 0 is dedicated to his memory.'

I read that dedication a second time, and then a third just to be certain, given that it seemed to imply his brother was dead. I put down the dissertation and went back over to my original notes. Had I made some sort of mistake? Were there two Tom Fields, one of whom had died during his childhood, and later another brother had come along and taken his dead brother's name?

No, no mistake.

Tom Field, his brother, was alive and well and studying music at King's College, Cambridge – and he too would later be charged with fraud regarding the events in Maids Moreton, for which he was found not guilty. Of course, you might claim that 'dedicated to his memory' does not necessarily mean that his brother had died, but I think it is reasonable to assume that most people reading that phrase would have interpreted it in this way. Poor Tom is no more, and good for his brother Ben to want to remember him. I recalled that Roger Perkins had described Field to me as a 'humblebragger'; he appeared to be humble but was in fact just drawing attention to himself. He liked to play games, but how should we interpret what this game might imply about his relationship with Tom?

Even in Chapter 0, the peculiarly named Introduction, Tom isn't let off the hook. After quoting Muldoon, that repetition and rhyme are not artificial – they are not imposed on the language, but are a deliberate and everyday part of language – Field mentions his brother again: 'Tom Field is a poet whose work fully deserves the praise it receives. It is worth noting at this point that his poetry receives no praise.' Poor Tom. I'm so pleased that I grew up with sisters, rather than a brother.

Let's now consider what the dissertation is all about. Who is Paul Muldoon and how does Field's interest in him help us to better understand his character and the way that he thinks? Perhaps it really does, in the words of his father, allow us an insight into Field's mind.

*

Paul Muldoon was born in Northern Ireland in 1951 and brought up on a farm in County Armagh. The *Times Literary Supplement* described him as one of the 'most significant English-language poets born since the Second World War'; he has acted as president of the Poetry Society and as poetry editor of the *New Yorker*. He was Professor of Poetry at Oxford between 1999 and 2004, and he won the Pulitzer Prize for Poetry in 2003. By any standards this is an extraordinarily impressive CV.

However, Muldoon remains a controversial poet and his work is seen as 'difficult': enigmatic and allusive; at times obscure, given the language he uses to express himself. He is fond of puns, riddles and wordplay, and so some have questioned how serious he is. Other critics, such as John McAuliffe, writing in the *Irish Times* in 2016, have suggested more darkly that words can be used 'not to include, but to divide and control one another'.

Not only was Field going to champion Muldoon's poetry, but to do so he was also going to employ a methodology called ergodicity. Put simply, ergodicity requires the reader to spend a significant period of time trying to understand the work. Field suggests that ergodicity is an 'experience' that allows the reader 'to choose how they read a work', as the writer is not the 'sole authority over the text, which continues being created after the work itself has left the writer's desk'.

So Field's dissertation is about a difficult poet, noted for his game-playing, riddles and obscure language. He then uses a methodology that attempts to deconstruct what that poet has written by prioritising the reader's (his own) subjective understanding of the text, rather than what the author might have originally intended. He is in effect insisting that the reader is not just contributing to the poem by analysing what it contains, and asserts that 'there is no distinction or inequality between the ability of the writer and the ability of the reader to create the text'. He sees ergodicity as a 'competitive sport' in which 'the reader is both performer and audience'.

This is not my academic world, and it is for others to make comment about Field's analysis. However, what he wrote seemed to resonate with his supervisor and more broadly within UB, so much so that they were prepared to have his dissertation published. Field's own clever wordplay within his text, his own games and riddles – is *he* being serious? – prompted by Muldoon's allusive style must have impressed, delighted and even dazzled. He'd clearly learned their language; like Frankenstein's monster, he'd watched and observed their rituals and their customs so that he could integrate and finally be accepted. He was Tom Ripley, dressing up in Dickie's clothes, mimicking his voice, parting his hair just so and watching himself in the mirror. He liked what he saw. But, at the end of the day, what did his dissertation actually add up to?

Criminologists are often accused, especially by psychologists, of being too reductionist. I am trying to avoid that trap but, to me, Field seems to be concluding that he is just as good at game-playing as Muldoon, and that ultimately he can take equal credit for his body of work, or indeed any other work he chooses to read. The reader, he argues, just as much as the author, creates the text; there is no inequality or distinction between the two. What's more, in the competitive sport of ergodicity, he is a champion; a winner; someone to admire. After all, he could use the right words and employ edgy methodologies. In short, he looked and sounded the part. Even so, all the time that I was reading his dissertation, Field felt to me like the literary equivalent of all those teenagers who practise singing in their bedrooms, a hairbrush for a microphone, and then audition for *The X Factor*. They're convinced that they're the next big thing and can hold a note or two; some might even convince Simon Cowell, but in reality they're superficial, not very talented, original or creative and, above all else, they lack authenticity.

I would suggest that all of this offers us an insight into Field's thinking and it's not a pleasant view. One final observation by his old journalism lecturer helped to confirm my thinking.

In our final interview, Roger Perkins recalled Field coming back to UB when he was in the process of writing his MA dissertation. One morning they happened to park their cars at the same time and walked over to the Chandos Building together. Roger remembered that he felt that he needed to be 'professional' around Field, and so was slightly on his guard.

'We were just walking into the university,' said Roger, 'and then Field, almost out of nowhere, said to me: "I really need fifty thousand words to express my thoughts, as opposed to your semi-autistic news haikus." I just laughed, but I thought, you're a right little fucker.' As he recounted their exchange, Roger looked away from me slightly, as if scanning the near distance, and then quietly said: 'Who's the semi-autistic news haiku now? Turns out it's you.'

I like Roger: no smoke, no mirrors, no, well, ergodicity.

Let's get back to criminology and the P-SCAN.

*

In assigning scores for each item of the P-SCAN, I look for evidence to support my allocation of 0, 1 or 2. Obviously there is a subjective element and how I might score could be different from how other people would score when considering the same evidence. This is sometimes called the problem of inter-rater reliability and which has become a whole subgenre when discussing the psychopathy checklist, and the P-SCAN more specifically. Those technical issues are for another day, and need not trouble us here. What I do need to do now is to show you some of the evidence I used in coming to my decision – I want to give you a flavour of some of my 'workings out'.

However, despite having conducted hundreds of P-SCANs, I am not implying that my individual, subjective expertise of working in this field gives me any greater right to assign a particular score; I am not trying to impose my decision from above. Rather, I want to justify my decision from the bottom up, by allowing you to see the evidence that I have collected and prioritised, and then how I have interpreted it.

It is also worth noting that I tend to seek evidence that

160

comes from sources that are independent of the individual under discussion; these types of sources are my 'gold standard'. I am less convinced by what the subject of the P-SCAN might say for all kinds of reasons – most obviously, they do not necessarily tell the truth, or they might have it in their interests to obfuscate and complicate. In the context of Field, for example, I constructed the P-SCAN prior to his appearance at court, but I later revised my scores when new independent evidence came to light at his trial. I tended to distrust what Field himself said in the witness box, which would often take one's breath away with its detached lack of insight. He had, after all, a very clear axe to grind and was constructing his answers to suit his own particular needs, in an attempt to prove his innocence.

Finally, it is worth remembering that I have spoken with a number of people who knew Field, read what his friends and acquaintances have said about him and, through my police contacts, have many of his emails and journal entries. As these were never intended for public consumption, I would suggest that they are probably closer to the truth than what he might later have been prepared to say in court. Finally, the 'workings out' that I am sharing here are meant to be illustrative – they are just a small part of the overall bank of evidence that I collected to construct the P-SCAN.

Let's consider three different types of evidence: a newspaper account of his various relationships; the sermon that he preached at his father's church in 2017, on the theme of 'Thou Shalt Not Kill'; and, finally, one of his journal entries about Peter. These sources allow us to construct the P-SCAN based on those facets of Field's underlying personality in relation to his interpersonal relations; what his emotional life might have been like; and his lifestyle. The first that I will discuss is a report from the ITV News website:

> Benjamin Field had a string of girlfriends while pretending to be in relationships with Peter Farquhar and Ann Moore-Martin.
>
> Field's complicated love life was explained in detail to the jury to illustrate a propensity to deceive and lie to people.
>
> He began seeing Lara Busby in late 2012, before splitting briefly in the summer of 2013, and resuming that October and continuing until 2017.
>
> In early 2013, Field had a brief fling with Heather Joyce, which lasted until the summer.
>
> His relationship with Mr Farquhar started in early 2013 and lasted until the lecturer's death in October 2015.
>
> For three months from February 2014, Field had a liaison with Nina Eriksen-Grey who he worked with at a nursing home.
>
> And in March 2014, Field began a fourth relationship, this time with Dr Setara Pracha, a University of Buckingham English literature lecturer, which lasted until his arrest.
>
> In early 2016, Field began a second fake relationship, this time with Mr Farquhar's neighbour, Miss Moore-Martin.
>
> While Field was seeing Miss Busby, Dr Pracha and Miss Moore-Martin, he had a one-night stand in June 2016 with Victoria Anderson.
>
> In 2010 and 2011, Field had been paid between £30 and £50 for receiving oral sex in hotels from men who answered

an ad he had placed on the 'casual encounters' section of the Craig[s]list website.

And in 2013, 2014 and 2016 he had further sexual encounters with men who he met via the Grindr social networking app – trysts he admitted lying to the jury about.

Field told jurors during his trial that the most important relationships in his life were with his parents, his brother and sister, and former girlfriend Dr Pracha.

'I have deceived absolutely everybody that I have any kind of relationship with,' he added.

Source: 'Benjamin Field's complicated love life showed his propensity to deceive', ITV News, 9 August 2019.

This first piece of evidence offers us an insight into the byzantine world of Field's personal relationships. From 2012 until the time of his conviction in 2019, he had at least four different relationships with women, including Dr Setara Pracha, who also taught English at UB, was his PhD supervisor and with whom he was living when he was taken into custody; he had been betrothed to Peter and established another relationship soon after his death with Ann Moore-Martin; and he was also regularly meeting men online. The number of these relationships, with both men and women, is in itself significant, but this complexity also provides us with a detailed understanding about how he must have presented himself interpersonally.

He had described himself as 'snake-talking' his way into Peter's home and affections, but this was not a one-off: it was clearly a fundamental part of his underlying personality; it was who he was. He had the gift of the gab and was a smooth-talker and so he would come across as self-confident and self-assured; he was a charmer. He was a 'humblebragger', to use Roger's phrase, and so he would always attempt to present himself in the best possible light when meeting people, and I get the distinct impression that this was the key to his success. He would also be able to take control and, if the occasion demanded, was adept at using grandiose language to try to impress other people. However, because he was like this, it would be difficult to actually get to know him. He would have been like a chameleon, able to adapt his language and his presentation of self to suit the person – male or female – he wanted to impress. That's why his former school friends thought of him as both being a 'loner' and having 'loads of friends'.

It is because of these facets of his underlying personality that he would have been able to establish so many relationships with people of both genders. He would have been skilled at gaining their trust, and just as adept at dropping them later. But how are we to account for the fact that some of these relationships overlapped with one another, and that some might have been long-term, while others were more fleeting and transitory? What might this also reveal about his interpersonal style?

The answer to these questions takes us back to the fundamental features of Field's personality, whether he was socialising in a group, or on a one-to-one basis. He would always have been opportunistic, and therefore looking for an advantage from any encounter, with either a man or a woman, that he could later use to benefit himself. So what, he would have reasoned, if he was already in another relationship? That might mean that some people would find him charismatic, while others would perhaps find it uncomfortable to be around him. A few people would positively dislike being in his company, as he would look for their weak spots in order to 'push their buttons' when he realised that he couldn't use them – with that type of person, he would just have wanted to dominate and be in charge. We glimpsed one example of that aspect of his interpersonal style when he walked with Roger from the car park to the Chandos Building. His joke that Roger, as a journalist, wrote 'semi-autistic news haikus' was deliberate; it was a condescending sneer that was meant to put him down and establish Field as his superior. We know that that was a trait of his personality even at school, where he would patronise some of his teachers by learning words from the dictionary that they could not possibly know.

As for being able to maintain parallel relationships, given that lying would come easily to him, his explanations for being late for an appointment, or not turning up for a meal that had perhaps been planned weeks in advance would have been superficially convincing. Even if in your heart of hearts you tended not to believe him, it would be difficult to actually check out what he was saying one way or another, as over the years he would have become skilled at avoiding ever being pinned down. Frankly, he would have been able to look you in the eye and assure you that night was day, that black was white, and that he really did love you – yes completely, and only you. I also get the impression that it was this skill that allowed him to be so persuasive about Peter's supposed 'declining health'.

The second piece of evidence relates to the sermon that Field would give while on bail for the murder of Peter.

'Thou Shalt Not Kill.' Some people say that we should not because it is illegal, or because it violates property rights, or other rights of the individual. But what about preventing death against a patient's consent, or will, or volition. Questions of medical ethics are just one area where it quickly gets difficult ... legally enforced norms are less important than one's personal convictions.

Source: Sermon preached by Ben Field at Olney Baptist Church, 29 October 2017 originally posted on church website, but since removed.

This sermon provides us with an insight into his emotional life – his feelings, his ability to show empathy, his guilt or remorse – which is more clinically called affect. It also tells us something about the sincerity of his religious views. It is important to remember that this sermon came just two years after the death of his partner who, we should not forget, he had murdered, and only five months after the death of Ann Moore-Martin, with whom he tried to establish a relationship. He would have been well aware that Miss Moore-Martin's family had shared their suspicions about him with the police, and that Peter's body had been exhumed on 30 May 2017. Field had also been arrested in March on suspicion of murder, and then bailed by the police. In other words, he knew that the police were asking questions not only about his relationship with Ann, but also about his relationship with Peter. He had also had to leave his job at the Red House Nursing Home, as a result of the police giving what was described to me as 'safeguarding advice' to their senior managers.

Of course, Field might have claimed it was these very experiences that entitled him to make informed comment on the biblical commandment 'Thou Shalt Not Kill'. However, it seems to me that there is much more going on here, with this deliberate, clerical sleight of hand, that allows us some understanding of his inner emotional life, and perhaps even more fundamentally his sense of self and entitlement. The temptation is simply to see his sermon as a sort of tasteless psychological dare he gave himself – go on, see if you can get away with this! In return, we might think to ask ourselves 'Is he serious?' or 'Perhaps this is just a terrible joke – an extreme example of bad taste?' For me, the answer to these questions is that he was serious: his message may have been inauthentic, but it is what he genuinely believed. He was being sincere, but had no true sense of how his sermon was inappropriate and offensive.

That, to put it mildly, should be of great concern.

The first thing to note is, given all of the context I have described, how unusually cool Field is under pressure. Someone with a greater sense of guilt, or with genuine feelings of remorse, would have been anxious, nervous, or even visibly distressed. The last thing they would have wanted to do is preach in church, knowing that what they said was to be recorded and made more widely available. Field does not have feelings like that because he really didn't have any strong emotional ties to any of the people he once claimed he loved, and so he can happily take to the pulpit.

Nor does he have any real concern for what he has done, for he simply does not believe or understand that it was wrong. His emotional life isn't peppered with right and wrong, or good and evil, because he doesn't think in the same way that you and I might. Murder was for him merely a way he could achieve his goals. Even the delivery of his sermon seemed to me flat, lacking in genuine emotion. In any event, he feels justified in what he has done and so can't really see why it would be so unusual to want to preach about this issue. He would have been puzzled that some people might have been upset by what he said, because that's not what he feels, or has ever felt.

The sermon also grants him permission. In the same way that he argues the reader of Muldoon's poetry has an equal part to play in the creation of the text, so too he wants to (re) create the sixth commandment. This is not really 'Thou Shalt Not Kill', but rather 'you can kill if you feel it is the right thing to do': he's using ergodicity again. This is not really a Christian narrative about how to live, or specifically about how to die, but at best a pick-and-mix spirituality. Field, in other words, is harvesting articles of moral teaching and elements of Christian belief to create his own bespoke flotsam-and-jetsam religion that suits his own personal needs and circumstances; as such, he really does believe what he is saying. In that sense, not only is he equal to Paul Muldoon, but he is also equal to God. His egotism is boundless. Of course, the difference with Christianity is that the fragments of belief he describes and prioritises have no underlying, compelling system of genuine faith to hold them together as a coherent and explicable whole; they are simply another means to an end.

I have questions about this sermon which I cannot answer definitively. Who was it, for example, that had asked him to deliver this sermon, or did Field himself offer to do so? Who chose the topic 'Thou Shalt Not Kill', had the sermon recorded and then posted it onto the church's website? As I say, I cannot answer these questions definitively but, in the same way that he kept notes and emails outlining exactly what he thought about Peter, I rather get the impression that the answer to these three questions would be Field himself.

All of this also makes me question his relationship with his family, especially with his father, the minister of the church where he is preaching. He is using his father's 'house' to make the most appalling of statements – or, to use a cruder idiom, he is shitting on his own doorstep. In one of his chat logs he notes 'I only ever talk about my dad, several ppl [sic] have noted this in conversations. I always write it off as my relationship w/mum [sic] is less conflicted, and, as such, less interesting.' I would suggest that there is a great deal of truth here – Field likes conflict, and specifically with his father. This thought also takes me back to *A Bitter Heart* and Rob being assured by his father that no one could ever suspect him of having committed a murder. Was that what Field had hoped for too, or was he simply testing how outrageous his behaviour could become before he would be caught out and censured?

More generally to what extent did his parents spend their lives covering up for Field and making excuses for him when he had done things like this before? Perhaps they had become adept at pouring oil on troubled waters, while all the time convincing themselves he would grow out of it. Remember his acknowledgement to his family in his thesis? He wanted to pay tribute to their 'tolerance ... across the period of time between my birth and now'.

Sadly, the way that he would have handled his relationship with his family would have been exactly the same as how he had managed interpersonal relationships with friends and other acquaintances. He would have used them for his own ends and would have had no genuine emotional attachment to them. Several family members – his parents and his brother included – were even on the list of people that he thought might be 'useful' to him that the police discovered after his arrest. In fact, that's why he felt entitled to preach his diabolical sermon in his father's church, and gives us another way of understanding his strange acknowledgement to his brother Tom.

Finally, we come to one of Field's journal entries about Peter:

Peter went from Boy's School to Cambridge to Boy's School. Not one scrap of an hour was unaccounted for across a five decade period. School furnished him with activity and society and importance and food and laundry and so on. Upon retirement he rattles around his house, not writing. Peter says he is slash [*sic*] wants to be a 'writer'. He is wrong. He wants to be an author. Peter does not enjoy writing, nor is he good at it, but he craves status and approval in a sickly dependant way, and *having written a book* can give him these things (in theory). Later in our friendship I edited his second novel for him, and suggested that we collaborate on a book. This is, once again, my own ambition seeking to exploit both Peter's vanity and his desire for companionship.

Source: Undated journal entry written by Ben Field.

Note the last three lines. He is making it clear that he is seeking to use Peter; his intentions are parasitic. He is trying to use their relationship to benefit himself and, as this entry reveals, he has no genuine feeling whatsoever for Peter. What he is displaying here is his sense of entitlement: he helped to edit Peter's book, so he now has the right to do as he pleases; this is about what he feels is by right his. Even so, he describes all of this, with no hint of irony, as 'our friendship'.

I believe that this entry gives us some insight into Field's lifestyle more generally: not just how he will use individuals, but also how he will use the institutions that he attaches himself to, such as UB and the church. However, of the three facets that make up the P-SCAN score, it was on this that Field scored lowest. To have scored more highly I would have expected to have uncovered issues in his background related to truancy, or having dropped out of school and consequently a poor academic record. But Field completed his secondary education and graduated from university. He was also regularly employed and so, while he might have been living rent-free at Peter's house, it is obvious, perhaps because of the influence of his family, that he was expected to find work and to be able to hold down a job. Nor did I discover that he had been constantly in trouble with the police; he was clearly no criminal mastermind, which is why I therefore also came to think of him as a less talented Tom Ripley.

However, I did note that his friends said he seemed to get bored easily, which we can perhaps see in the burglaries he admitted to in court and in his desire to initiate covert sexual liaisons. These must have been exciting, as well as satisfying his sexual interests. Of course when dealing with people like Field there are no simple answers. So, even if he did defraud Ann and benefited financially from Peter's will, he was not, as far as I could determine, living life in the fast lane but rather modestly – he didn't want to stand out in that way.

As for his other scores, the facet of the P-SCAN on which Field scored highest was concerned with his interpersonal relations. Of the thirty questions that made up this facet, he scored on twenty-five of them. A high score suggests that the person takes a dominant and controlling stance during actions with other people, and that they are likely to be 'grandiose, egocentric, manipulative, deceptive, conning and perhaps charming in a superficial way. Such a person views himself as the centre of the universe, with a well-established sense of entitlement.' Someone who scores high on this facet is also likely to be a smooth-talking con artist, given to playing head games, and what they say should never be taken at face value.

I will not provide my individual scores or indeed, for ethical reasons, Field's total P-SCAN score but, suffice to say, it was well within the high range, and I described at the start of this chapter what that implies. In this respect, he was on par with several serial killers I have interviewed and, perhaps more memorably for me as my encounters were filmed, with Bert Spencer, a convicted murderer who I interviewed for a Channel 4 documentary about his possible role in the murder of the schoolboy Carl Bridgewater in 1978. So if I had been in a situation where I had to manage Field, or if he had written back to me and I had got the opportunity to interview him, I would have known that I could not trust anything he said. I would also have expected him to attempt to manipulate and control me. The form that control would most likely take would be for him to try to toady and ingratiate, rather than be openly hostile and aggressive. However, I have no doubt that if he felt he needed to, he could use violence, or the threat of violence. After all, this is a man capable of murder.

*

I've never particularly favoured an approach that attempts to 'look into the mind' of an offender, and have always rather distrusted those people who do. I prefer to consider and analyse an offender's behaviour, which, of course, probably does relate to their thoughts, feelings and emotions. Action is after all related to how people think. However, considering an individual's behaviour seems to me a much more empirical basis on which to come to a conclusion about them, rather than speculating as to what they fantasise about, or how they think more generally. There is certainly a place for analysing thoughts, feelings and emotions once the offender is in therapy, but that is not where we currently are with Field.

It seems fair to conclude that Field's behaviour was predatory and calculating, and that he had no sense of guilt, shame or remorse for the consequences of that behaviour. Ben Field was out for himself – both in terms of the individuals he met and befriended and, having learned their customs, cultures and systems, also within the institutions he attached himself to. He was going to attempt to ingratiate himself to reach the top, all the time believing that he was entitled to get there anyway. He thought he deserved all the glittering prizes on offer, which were, he would have reasoned, his by right. His sense of entitlement came not just from his belief about who he thought himself to be, but also because he would perform roles within these institutions. He would take seminar groups at UB, for example, and act as deputy warden at Stowe Parish Church. And with Peter, he had helped to edit his book.

Field saw all of this as a *quid pro quo*, although he also noted in his chat log that 'I dunno [*sic*] what goes on in my head most of the time'. Let's not be persuaded by that and simply accept Roger's assessment: he was just 'a right little fucker'.

Field's P-SCAN score suggests to me that he had behaved in this way for a very long time, and that without significant help he will continue to behave in this way for the rest of his life. He will therefore not be easy to manage in prison – not because he will riot, or take hostages but because he'll charm and manipulate both staff and other prisoners to get them to do his bidding. He will use them just as much as he used Peter.

All of this suggests to me that Field was not just capable of one murder, but would have continued to do so whenever the opportunity arose; once the genie was out of the bottle, he would be unable to put it back in again. As his sermon made clear, the sixth commandment could be reinterpreted, permitting him to kill whenever he deemed it necessary, because 'legally enforced norms are less important than one's personal convictions'. And Field's personal convictions were strong; he believed every word he said. Ever the narcissist, his ego was infinite. We must take that chilling statement very seriously: he had killed once and, as the aphorism goes, the best indication of future behaviour is past behaviour.

It was now time for the police and jury to consider that behaviour.

CHAPTER EIGHT

Operation Naseby

'Not very often you bail a murderer'

Senior Investigating Officer MARK GLOVER,
quoted in *Catching a Killer: A Diary from
the Grave*, Channel 4, 13 January 2020

The town of Kidlington is a flat, ugly sprawl of bungalows and two-up, two-downs that seem to go on forever in one long, endless straight line as far as the eye can see. It's a planning and architectural accident of cheap housing that capitalises on its closeness to the city of Oxford, but which is devoid of beauty, or anything even remotely pleasing to look at. If Hell exists, it will resemble Kidlington. I'm sure that the people who live there are decent folk who love one another, care about their kids and pay their taxes, and those residents I spoke to were unfailingly kind and friendly, but how they manage to cope with the town's unrelenting ugliness is beyond me.

Perhaps I saw it on a bad day.

Kidlington is also the home of the Thames Valley Police (TVP) Headquarters, and I was over an hour early for my appointment with Mark Glover, the Senior Investigating Officer (SIO) on Peter's case, which had been named Operation Naseby. Naseby is a village in Northamptonshire, best known as the site of a Civil War battle in 1645.

I thought that I would find somewhere to sit down and have a coffee, so took refuge in Costa on Kidlington's high street. It gave me an opportunity to look over my notes and prepare for the interview. In particular, I ran through what I had written about the Channel 4 documentary on the case, called *Catching a Killer: A Diary from the Grave*, which had aired at the start of 2020. It was a painful and distressing watch that showed the realities of investigating murder, and had briefly become the talk of Buckingham and Maids Moreton.

I hadn't actually started out wanting to interview Mark for this book at all, but I had recently given a lecture on contract killers at the TVP's annual research conference, and everyone thought it would be a good idea if we made contact. I was undecided. Senior police officers have better things to do with their time than speak with academics writing books, but, if I am being honest, there was more to my hesitation than concerns about wasting police time. Over the years, I have become tired of 'police speak', and the rehearsed rhythms and cadences of the answers that flow from a generic policing and detective culture that is instinctively defensive and insular. Even if I am an informed outsider who has helped with live investigations, cold cases and police training, I am not an insider, so they are always going to be cautious about what they say to me.

I knew I would be treated courteously, but I wasn't sure that I would learn anything I didn't already know. What was there to be gained from talking with the SIO who had led the investigation?

My unease wasn't helped by viewing *Catching a Killer: A Diary from the Grave*. This was unashamedly the police procedural approach, which is familiar to drama audiences and often repackaged as true crime. True crime was memorably described by Professor Mark Seltzer of UCLA as 'crime fact that looks like crime fiction' and, as a genre, one that sought to display and capitalise on the torn bodies of our 'wound culture'. In exactly the same way as *MasterChef* or *Strictly Come Dancing* are products designed to show off the skills of the chefs or the dancers, this true crime documentary was consciously constructed to reassure us that the police really were our capable, professional guardians who keep the barbarians at the gate. The documentary was a dark, gruesome form of entertainment, even if it did allow us a partial glimpse of what a police murder investigation looks like.

I knew from my conversations with people in Buckingham and Maids Moreton that they were shocked by what they saw in the documentary. At one point, Peter's exhumed body is seen on the mortuary table and Dr Brett Lockyer, the forensic pathologist, says enthusiastically of his hair, 'very well preserved, yes, very well preserved'. For a brief moment we even seen Peter's dead body, lying on the sofa in his house. In my work as a criminologist I have of course been privy to these types of incidents and conversations, but I too was shocked by the documentary, which felt both authentic and yet staged and artificial at the same time. It made me uneasy.

I should of course acknowledge that I do not know the specifics of the agreement between the TVP and True Vision, the production company who made the documentary for Channel 4. However, I have little doubt that any flaws in their investigation, mistakes that were made, blind alleys that were walked down, or any unprofessional behaviour that might have been captured by the film crew would have been left on the cutting-room floor. I don't know if what was being filmed was stage-managed, or perhaps even scripted. Were we seeing and hearing things that had been filmed in real time, or reconstructed when the light, the sound, or even what was said, were better? From my own TV work I know, above all, that the version the viewer would see would be a picture of dogged determination, stoicism in the face of adversity, tenacity, perseverance, kindness, and a relentless pursuit of the truth. I would like to think that all murder investigations are like that, but I know that they're not. What *Catching a Killer: A Diary from the Grave* presented was a carefully and artfully created product telling a version of a murder investigation in the best possible way.

Even so, there were a few glaring holes that left me with a number of questions. I wondered whether I should raise these with Mark, after deciding that it would be rude not to make contact having been encouraged to do so. How had Mark felt, for instance, when Martyn Smith had been acquitted of all the charges that had been brought against him, and that Tom Field had also been found not guilty? After all, pursuit of Smith and Field's brother had been part of his investigation. Why also, if Field had jumped out of the window of the flat that he was sharing with Dr Setara Pracha on the night that he was arrested, had she never been interviewed, or called as a witness? Exactly how was Field 'being monitored' by the police, as was stated on several occasions in the documentary, and what was the basis of the dark hints that were made about Field and other 'unexplained murders' in the Buckingham area?

Finally, I thought that even the title was more than a little disingenuous. This was hardly an investigation that hinged on a diary from the grave, for in reality everything relied on developments in forensic science and the skills of the pathologist.

At Field's trial, which wasn't in the documentary, Dr Lockyer stated that Peter had been repeatedly exposed to the drugs flurazepam, diclazepam, lorazepam and flubromazolam. He concluded that 'the combination of flurazepam and alcohol is likely to have resulted in potentation of the sedative effects of both substances and may have proved fatal through decreasing the level of consciousness and posing a threat to an adequate airway'. Dr Lockyer also stated that there may have been 'third-party interference with the normal mechanics of breathing' – by which he means suffocation – and that the cause of death was poisoning over 'at least a six-month period'.

Just as well, then, that there had been a body to exhume. Frankly, if Peter had been cremated Field would still be a free man. That was why Mark had to release Field on bail: he needed the forensic evidence to charge him with murder, as his emails, chat logs and notebooks and Peter's journals were just not enough. Yet even with 886 statements, more than two thousand police exhibits and all the forensic evidence that had been gathered, it still took the jury twenty-four days to come to a decision.

The police did get their man in the end, though.

*

I left Costa somewhat reluctantly and started to walk back along the unsightly scar that masquerades as Kidlington's main road, in the direction of Oxford and the police HQ.

After about twenty minutes, I found myself walking through a spacious police car park and into the main building.

I approached the reception desk and, with my practised smile, explained who I was and gave the name of the person I had come to see. I knew that none of this information would make any difference whatsoever. All receptionists in the various institutions of the criminal justice system are, it seems, professionally required to claim not to be able to find your name on their list of approved visitors. However, more worryingly, on this occasion one asked me, 'Do you know what Mark Glover does?' Perhaps they hadn't watched the documentary. Anyway, their questions made me conscious that I was being put through some form of oral examination that I needed to pass.

Keeping my smile firmly in place, I explained that Mark was a detective, but even armed with this information they were still struggling to locate him, or me, and so they tried another angle: 'Do you know who's organised the meeting?'

Having spent years gaining access to similar secure buildings, I knew this was my trump card. I did know, and promptly gave them the name of a press officer.

That seemed to have the desired effect.

Naturally the receptionist was slightly deflated as he handed me a visitor's badge, and directed me towards a seat.

'We've asked him to come and pick you up here. It should only be ten minutes.'

I sat down in front of a large notice board, which had photographs of all the senior police officers arranged in strict rank hierarchy. At the top was John Campbell, the Chief Constable, and then, below him, Deputy Chief Constable Jason Hogg, and thereafter the various assistant chief constables. Everyone was smiling; most were male. The board also contained some basic information: that the Thames Valley Police, which covers Berkshire, Buckinghamshire and Oxfordshire, an area of over 2200 square miles, with a population of 2.1 million people, and employs more than 4000 police constables and over 2500 police staff. Their motto is *Sit Pax in Valle Tamesis* – 'Let there be Peace in the Thames Valley', and their corporate tagline is 'Serving with Pride and Confidence'. Smiling. Serving. Pride. Confidence. Everything had an air of corporate efficiency and managerial competence; 'you are safe in our hands' was the message, or at least that's what they wanted to sell – just like the documentary.

The press officer duly arrived after ten minutes, followed by Mark Glover. He was about my height, thin and wiry; he didn't make eye contact as we shook hands. I exchanged pleasantries with him about scenes in the documentary where he had been riding his motorbike. For the first time, Mark smiled.

I'd done a bit of research about his career and so I knew that Mark had joined the police when he was twenty, and had reached the rank of Detective Chief Inspector, before retiring after thirty years' service in May 2018. He had returned to the TVP a month later as a civilian investigator. During his career he had worked on child exploitation cases and kidnaps, and had had a wealth of experience in investigating rapes, manslaughters and murders. He'd also had experience of working with the TVP's Serious Organised Crime Unit and the drugs squad.

The press officer ushered us into an empty room and, given Mark's impressive CV, I began by asking how the investigation into Peter's death had compared to other cases he had worked. Mark started to answer by describing his experience of murder more generally:

> Most murders are five minutes of madness, but this wasn't. It was planned over a long period of time and with a great deal of preparation. It was unlike any investigation that I have previously worked on in my thirty-one years of police service.

I smiled as Mark told me this, nodded, and like a good academic duly wrote down what he said. The press officer also seemed to be noting down what I asked and how Mark replied. My smiling, and my previous comments about Mark on his motorbike, were an attempt to establish some form of personal rapport; to try to say, 'it's OK, you can trust me'. However, Mark's answer to my first tentative question was an almost verbatim echo of the TVP's press release at the end of the case – I remembered the 'five minutes of madness' line. He had actually been more forthcoming in the documentary, when he stated that the investigation had been 'a once-in-a-lifetime type of case that you would investigate as an SIO'. I started to worry again, wondering just how valuable my interview was going to be. There was nothing left to lose, I thought, so I decided to ask one of my harder questions.

'Were you surprised,' I said, 'that Smith was found not guilty?' Mark seemed unfazed and was frank in his reply, although his opinion was given in confidence. However, we discussed various theories about the case and the relationships that had developed between different parties.

I shared with him that I had recently seen Smith back in Buckingham. Seemingly he was keen to restart his studies at the university, although I was later told that he had been advised to do so via distance learning. Sharing this information from my own research seemed to put Mark more at ease, and we began to have a more open discussion, although we agreed that some of what we said to each other had to be off the record. However, we did discuss Field's relationships with Setara Pracha and with his parents, and the strange controversy around labelling Field a psychopath.

This label had apparently been applied to Field by a psychotherapist called Stephen Bushell. Bushell had been contracted by the Church of England to assess Field prior to his going forward to a Bishop's Advisory Panel (BAP), the final stage of the discernment process before being accepted for three years of ordination training. The Church stated that it 'did not receive a clinical diagnosis of psychopathic behaviour' about Field, but it admitted that 'serious concerns' had begun to emerge, although no one had thought he had been 'dangerous'. Nonetheless, despite these serious concerns, Field was going to be allowed to attend the BAP, with the possibility that he would be found suitable for ordination training. In the documentary Mark stated quite clearly that 'the psychotherapist had concerns that Field could be a psychopath', and Bushell's report, using that term, had been read into the court record.

I wondered if this was an embarrassment for the Church of England, or for Bushell. The latter had flatly refused to speak with me, but there were obviously two possibilities:

first, I wondered if Bushell had perhaps not offered a clinical diagnosis about Field, which would then explain the Church's later position; or, second, if Bushell was not in fact qualified to offer a clinical diagnosis in the first place. I could find no Stephen Bushell in the list of chartered members on the British Psychological Society's website, nor on their register for psychologists specialising in psychotherapy. He was, however, listed with the UK Council for Psychotherapy as an 'Analytical Psychologist – Jungian Analyst'. Perhaps in his assessment Bushell had simply wanted to indicate that Field had several of the traits of psychopathy, but to have labelled him as such might have been beyond his professional training and experience. It is all a bit of a mystery and not one that I am able to fully solve, although I find it difficult to accept that the Church would simply lie.

In other words, I do not think they had received a clinical diagnosis of psychopathy.

Even so, it is obvious that the Church still had questions it needed to answer about its discernment process.

I was able to discuss quite openly with Mark Glover what his views were about Field, and whether he would have killed other people. There was the tantalising statement he had made in the documentary, that he had been worried about 'the deaths of other elderly people in the Buckingham area'. Who were these elderly people? There was also Field's list of a hundred names to consider, although later he would describe it as simply being a list of people who might be 'useful' to him. By this, Field claimed in court, he meant he could live with them for free, or defraud them in various ways. His brother Tom was on the list, as were his parents and the mother of

Setara Pracha. Was this list, in Mark's view, simply about those people who could be 'useful' to Field, or did it have more sinister implications? Mark said:

> The danger here was that he would kill a hundred. He claimed it wasn't about murder, but fraud and theft. But I think that his greed would have got the better of him. He should have stopped after killing Peter, but he was greedy. He'd have killed other people. He killed for greed and the pleasure that he got from it. Ben Field was all about Ben Field.

Mark's major concern was about Field's access to elderly people, who were his preferred victims. He said that it was the police's fears that Field would have 'killed again' which resulted in them engaging the Red House Nursing Home in safeguarding training, which led to Field losing his job.

However, he was less forthcoming about others in the Buckingham area who he felt had either been targeted by Field, or could have been murdered by him. In the Channel 4 documentary, Elizabeth Zettl was interviewed, because a copy of the front page of her will was discovered to be in Smith's possession, and we know from what was said at court that he had once lodged with the elderly lady. We also know that in court Field, but not Smith, admitted to breaking into the home of Peter's elderly neighbours, Mr and Mrs Meakin, who died before Field came to trial. Field also admitted to stealing from Jonathan Elliman, who was one of Peter's friends. In their text messages to each other, Smith and Field referred to Mr Elliman as 'the Jelliman'.

It was never mentioned during my interview with Mark, during the trial, or in the subsequent reporting about the case, but Field also had access to elderly people in the congregation at Stowe Parish Church – an access that would only have become easier if, or when, he started his ordination training.

I discussed two other areas with Mark. First, why did people in Maids Moreton and Buckingham not intervene? Second, did Mark ever consider the last novel Peter wrote as a sort-of blueprint for his murder? If I was right on that latter point, then stealing the plot of Peter's novel was Field's final, deadly way to betray Peter and display his own brilliance, cunning and intellectual acumen.

Mark thought that the answer to the first question was related to Field's credibility. 'He came across as credible; he was a student; he was involved with the church.' It was because of this credibility that he was then able to 'sell the narrative about Peter's alcoholism and dementia'. He also 'isolated Peter', and Mark saw Field's buying a dog as merely another way to maintain that isolation; the dog kept Peter at home; if, when he was able, he went out it was to take Kipling for a walk, rather than to visit friends. However, above all, it was the narrative that Field sold about Peter's supposed alcoholism and dementia that deflected attention from what was actually happening at 3 Manor Park. It was only after Peter's death that people started to come forward, whispering that they weren't sure the stories Field had spread had been true. By then it was too late.

Remember again how Harold Shipman had operated. Very few people had questioned the doctor's clinical behaviour, even if the elderly people who died in his care had been fit and well prior to Shipman visiting. Everyone had simply accepted his word; after all, he was a doctor. This was all about who has a voice – who has status within a community, and how that status is constructed, maintained and then enhanced. Shipman enhanced his status by being the only doctor in the community prepared to do home visits, which gave him the access he needed to his elderly patients.

Field built his status through connections with the church, his work at the nursing home, his relationship with a man already respected within the community, and through his academic achievements at UB. This last source should not be underestimated in a town that valued education, and I was intrigued that he had even told the custody sergeant at the time of his arrest that his occupation was 'author'. What had he meant by this? Was this the published MA dissertation, or was he mirroring Peter's status as an author and claiming it for himself? He had proofread *A Bitter Heart* and contributed 'necessary emendations' and so, in a *quid pro quo*, he seemed to believe that he was now an author too.

There is another tantalising possibility to consider here. Field, just as Tom Ripley 'became' Dickie Greenleaf, might be suggesting that he had become Peter Farquhar – an author and a scholar. This might be pushing the analysis too far, but it doesn't seem too fanciful to suggest that Field simply being motivated by greed doesn't quite capture the range of colours that we see displayed on the palette of his crimes.

Mark did not think that Peter knew about Field's true murderous intentions, because he'd never said outright 'Ben is poisoning me' in any of his journals. However, Mark had never read any of Peter's books and we agreed that, as Field often read Peter's journals, what he wrote in them might have been carefully edited and that he might not even have recorded some issues at all. Mark conceded that Peter probably 'understood Ben's character', that he was 'perceptive' and that Peter would sometimes confront Field about what he had written in his diaries, but 'he did change his will and so while I think that he understood Ben, I don't think that he knew what Ben was doing to him physically'.

I shared with Mark my reading of *A Bitter Heart*, but we had no meeting of minds on what it might imply. Time was pressing and I had only one further question, which related to the court case.

Was he surprised that the jury had taken so long to reach a verdict? He smiled, but repeated his view that it had been a complex case and so the jury had had a great deal to consider. This, he felt, was explanation enough for their twenty-four days of deliberations.

It was only after I had left the Thames Valley Police HQ that I started to reconsider why the investigation had been called Operation Naseby. Naseby was the site of a famous Parliamentarian victory in the English Civil War. However, the city of Oxford had been a Royalist stronghold and it was only after Sir Thomas Fairfax had abandoned his siege of the city to join forces with Oliver Cromwell that the Parliamentarians had won the day.

Is it pushing the analogy too much to suggest that the TVP were the Roundheads and Oxford Crown Court the Cavaliers?

CHAPTER NINE

Oxford Crown Court

'Most of my pleasures have been privately
held. It's a habit of a lifetime to be living
inside my head'

Ben Field's testimony

The trial of The Queen v Benjamin Luke Field, Martyn Smith and Tom Field began on 30 April 2019 at Oxford Crown Court in St Aldate's. The Crown Court had moved into the building which had once been the showroom for Morris Motors after the old Crown Court, located beside the prison, closed down in 1985. HMP Oxford itself limped on for another decade, before it too closed down and was eventually turned into a rather swanky hotel – part of the Malmaison chain. (It never ceases to amaze me that 'malmaison' is French for 'sick house'.) The trial was expected to last between six and twelve weeks, with the Honourable Mr Justice Sweeney presiding. Oliver Saxby, QC would appear for the prosecution, assisted by Michael Roques and Mark Davies, and David Jeremy, QC for the defence.

In total, there were eight counts on the indictment: murder, conspiracy to murder, attempted murder, fraud x 3, burglary and possession of an article used in fraud. This final charge was concerned with Elizabeth Zettl's will; the burglary charges related to thefts from Mr and Mrs Meakin at 5 Manor Park and from the home of Jonathan Elliman; and, finally, Tom Field was only charged with fraud in relation to one count – after Ann Moore-Martin had given Field money in the mistaken belief that his brother Tom was in desperate need of kidney dialysis.

The QCs, Oliver Saxby and David Jeremy, were both ranked by Chambers and Partners, the specialist firm that provides legal market intelligence, as Band 2 in their profession. Band 1 in this ranking system is the highest and Band 6 the lowest. Saxby, who had only become a QC in 2013, was nominated for Crime Silk of the Year in 2019 and was described as 'enjoying a reputation as an outstanding advocate' and 'incredibly thorough in his cross-examination'. David Jeremy, who had been a QC for much longer than Saxby, was particularly noted for having:

A reputation for straight dealing with clients, opponents and judges. He is the 'go-to' barrister for a demanding solicitor and a difficult case. His experience of prosecuting, defending and sitting as a recorder gives him a perspective and tactical advantage that can be used to transform a criminal trial. His ability to identify early the decisive issues in a case means that he knows which points to make and which to concede.

I knew this aspect of Mr Jeremy's advocacy from an older case, when in 2011 he had defended Danilo Restivo for the murder of his neighbour Heather Barnett nine years earlier. Restivo was an extremely strange, seemingly shambolic Italian who lived in England and who was also a trichophiliac – he had a sexual fetish for hair. He had bludgeoned Heather to death with a hammer, cut off her breasts and placed a lock of hair which did not belong to her in her right hand, and some of Heather's own hair under her left. As these brief details suggest, it was all very, very peculiar. At the trial it seemed as if Mr Jeremy was actually cross-examining his own client, and in his closing address to the jury he described Restivo as 'a deeply unattractive oddity, but that does not make him a killer'.

Despite these efforts, Restivo was found guilty.

Field's trial would last for seventy-seven days and, as previously mentioned, the jury deliberated for twenty-four of them. Given that Martyn Smith and Tom Field were found not guilty, I will only describe the trial from the perspective of Field, and will select specific days that seem to illuminate broader issues I have discussed, or need to be considered further. I attended the trial on one day, Tuesday 11 June, when I knew that Field would take the witness stand. I kept notes of what was said that day, and use these and the reporting of a local journalist called Sam Dean, who at the time worked for the *Bucks Herald*, to flesh out what happened on other days.

I noted Sam's attendance during my research into the court case. He filed copy for over thirty days during the trial, well beyond what normally happens within media reporting of court cases, which is usually focused on the opening day of the trial and on sentencing. I contacted Sam and he was happy to share with me his filed reports and, just as importantly, his memories of the days he attended court.

The days I will focus on are: Day 1 of the trial on 1 May and Mr Saxby's setting out of the prosecution case; Day 22, 11 June, when Ben Field is giving evidence; Day 23, 12 June, when Field talks about poetry and literature, and his betrothal to Peter; and finally the defence and prosecution summaries. I use direct quotes below from what was said in court by the various participants, although for ease of reference these are occasionally run together, especially when I offer highlights from closing arguments:

Day 1: Mr Saxby – 'This case concerns the murder of a sixty-nine-year-old man, Peter Farquhar and the attempted murder of an eighty-three-year-old woman, Ann Moore-Martin. The motive was financial gain laced with controlling, manipulating, humiliating and killing. They deceived the victim into changing their wills to inherit their houses. To achieve this the victims had to die and the defendants had to get away with it. For Ben Field this was a project. It was to befriend the victims, get them to change their wills and make sure that they died.'

Day 22: Ben Field is in the witness stand and Mr Jeremy asks him to confirm that he had fraudulently sought to benefit from the wills of Peter Farquhar and Ann Moore-Martin. He agreed that he had, to which Mr Jeremy then replied, 'So where's the lie?' Field states: 'The essence of the lie was that I loved him and that his feelings beyond the platonic were reciprocated by me. They were not.' As for the gaslighting, this was done 'to irritate him. I did it vindictively'. He admits to defrauding Ann Moore-Martin and when asked what he did with the money he states, 'Well I certainly didn't buy a dialysis machine.' He admits to the burglaries. He denies everything to do with murder and attempted murder. Finally he admits that 'I have deceived absolutely everyone that I've ever had a relationship with. I think that the most common kind of deception with me is to pretend that I am other than I am – that I'm better. I feel inadequate so it's pleasing to be someone else.'

Day 23: Ben Field is still in the witness stand discussing his 'rap battles' – another form of his writing that was disclosed by the police as well as his poetry, chat logs and so forth, his love of literature more generally and his betrothal to Peter. He agrees that they had often 'communicated with each other via this medium [literature and poetry] and Field suggests that his rap was 'a bit of sport. I'm not a writer of nice things. I don't enjoy positive types of writing – that's not interesting to me'. He is asked to explain 'a long-running literary debate he had with Mr Farquhar over what was to be most valued in literature – was it the message of a text, the moral substance, its meaning, or was it simply the quality of the language and the wordplay?' Field explains that he is in the 'latter camp of this debate while Peter Farquhar was in the former'. Field agrees that this is 'style over substance'. He also explains that on the day of his proposal he had bought cigars and dessert wine to make 'a fake event' and when questioned as to why that would be satisfying he replies, '[It's] pleasing knowing more than anyone else; feeling in charge – that you've got something on everyone else.' He adds: 'Most of my pleasures have been privately held. It's a habit of a lifetime to be living inside my head.' When he's challenged whether what he has said is true, he replies, 'These are true words, sincerely spoken.'

Closing argument edited highlights: Mr Saxby for the Prosecution: 'This case isn't about advocates. It isn't about the personalities. It's about the evidence; these were real plans with real victims, involving face-to-face deceit. Some of the things he's admitted doing are almost beyond belief. [Ben Field] is greedy in terms of power and self-importance; a sadist who inflicted pain because he enjoyed it; [someone] capable of casting a spell on people.' Mr Jeremy for the Defence: 'I regard it as a privilege to represent Ben Field. The fact is that based on the medical evidence Peter Farquhar could have died from taking his normal dose of flurazepam and drinking too much. They were two odd people united in their oddness. The truth in this case may not be Ben Field's truth but it is demonstrably not the prosecution's truth either.'

It is important to establish what it was that the jury would eventually come to accept as true – namely, that Field had murdered Peter Farquhar, and that the motive for that murder had been financial gain. This is the simple proposition that Mr Saxby outlines on Day 1 of the case, and he would return to that proposition in his summation. The jury accepted that proposition as fact. Of course, Saxby was also going to talk about control, manipulation and humiliation, and suggest that this was a 'project' for Field, which had involved him first befriending, then duping and finally killing his victims. And while the jury would, in the end, not find Field guilty of Ann Moore-Martin's murder, they did accept this basic summary of the case with regards to what happened to Peter.

Mr Saxby's job was not only to simplify for the jury, but also to present a robust enough account of the case to withstand the various denials and obfuscations that would inevitably come when Field's defence was presented. Our legal system is adversarial rather than inquisitorial; it is based on offering a narrative, either confirming or disputing the evidence collected by the police of what happened. The prosecution and the defence each hope that their narrative is more persuasive than the account that will be offered by the other side. I have described how the jury would come to accept the prosecution's narrative as 'fact' and, more than that, 'beyond reasonable doubt' – the standard of proof in a criminal trial. Ben Field, in other words, murdered Peter Farquhar. The more interesting jurisprudential question is the relationship between the facts that are produced in this way, and the truth.

Truth would be something that Mr Jeremy would return to on a number of occasions throughout the trial and, in his summing up for the defence before the jury were allowed to retire to consider their verdict, he specifically argues that: 'the truth in this case may not be Ben Field's truth but it is demonstrably not the prosecution's truth either.' In other words, it was not possible to determine beyond reasonable doubt what was true. Mr Jeremy caught something of the zeitgeist in all of this, as the truth no longer seems plain and simple for our generation and there are some who would claim that it does not exist at all – it is all a matter of opinion.

Mr Saxby, in turn, told the jury that the case hadn't been about 'advocates' or 'personalities' – even though he had crossed swords with Field on a couple of occasions – but about the evidence that had been presented. He reminded the jury that 'these were real plans with real victims, involving face-to-face deceit'. In the adversarial theatre of the court he persuaded his audience that his narrative was true and so won the argument, although it was clearly a close-run thing.

Day 22 saw Ben Field take the witness stand, and it was also the day that I was able to attend court. I was intrigued by the thought that Field was going to give evidence and wanted to see how he presented himself. My first impression was that he was physically much larger than I had imagined him to be from the photographs I had seen. He did not seem to be particularly anxious when he gave evidence, and looked around the rather poky court making eye contact with various people as he did so, almost as if he was seeking their approval. The court wasn't particularly busy, and I noted that there was a middle-aged couple in the public gallery, sitting close to me, who I now realise must have been Field's parents.

Rather than being on trial for murder, Field came across like a rather cocksure student in a seminar – one who had done all the reading, worked out everything for himself, and was now going to dazzle us all with his brilliance.

Even going into the witness stand was, in my experience, unusual for someone accused of murder. It was up to the prosecution to make their case – and so why run the risk, the defendants seem to reason, of jeopardising everything by being caught out by a clever prosecution barrister? I remember the serial killer Peter Tobin doodling with disinterest in a notebook during his trial at Chelmsford Crown Court in 2009, only looking up once throughout the entire proceedings, when his former wife entered the court to give evidence. He stared at her from the moment she came into the court until she sat down in the witness box, before returning to his doodling. His stares were probably the best insight I could gain into what their relationship had been like.

Murderers are usually silent and uncommunicative, especially about the murders that they have committed, and so Field was again unusual in that he wanted to personally put his case to the jury. Of course, that might simply have been another feature of his arrogance and narcissism in that he believed he could persuade them of his innocence in the same way that he believed he could outsmart the Church.

We also see on this day the tactic that Mr Jeremy is noted for in his defence – he is able to 'identify early the decisive issues in a case which means that he knows which points to make and which to concede'. At the plea and trial preparation hearing (PTPH), which had taken place in March 2019 via video-link from HMP Peterborough, where he was on remand, Field had indicated that he would plead guilty to the frauds and the burglaries; it was the more serious charges that he would deny. His admitting the burglaries and especially the frauds explains why Mr Jeremy asks, 'So, where's the lie?' This was an attempt to do two things. First, to show that Field could be relied upon to tell the truth. If he can admit to the frauds, this reasoning suggests, he must therefore also be telling the truth when he denies murder. It was also the start of a more difficult process of attempting to explain that what he had done to Peter was not an attempt to kill him, but rather the result of Field's underlying, and rather difficult and odd, personality. Field had wanted to irritate Peter and was being vindictive, but he was not a killer.

Field admits that 'the essence of the lie was that I loved [Peter]' when he did not, and that this was how he had behaved 'with absolutely everyone that I've ever had a relationship with'. He concedes that he likes to think that he's better than he really is, but explains that this is because he is 'inadequate so it's pleasing to be someone else'.

This is strong stuff, but even when I heard it being delivered in court I just didn't believe what Field was saying. It took my breath away, in that it appeared to be an authentic and honest self-assessment, but it came across as a carefully constructed lie that helped him out of a difficult spot. Perhaps years of listening to the stories that serious offenders have told me has made me jaundiced, but it struck me as another aspect of Field's underlying psychopathy and, later in my research, as yet another form of 'humblebragging'. He wanted to appear 'inadequate' to garner the jury's sympathy, as a rather sophisticated form of manipulation and deceit. His performance in court was not that of a man who thought himself 'inadequate';

the words he was using and his behaviour did not match. In one sense he's trying to suggest that he is suffering from a form of what psychologists call cognitive dissonance – that he is experiencing mental discomfort because he holds two conflicting beliefs: he presents himself as confident but secretly knows that he is imperfect and incomplete. Even so, in the witness box, and especially when being cross-examined, he would spar with Mr Saxby as his equal – if not his superior.

What's more interesting to consider is that if Field genuinely recognised that he had 'deceived absolutely everyone that I've ever had a relationship with', why could he not also recognise that he was attempting to deceive everyone in the court too? Perhaps he did.

This question comes up again the following day. Mr Jeremy asks Field if what he is saying is the truth, and he replies: 'These are true words, sincerely spoken.' This was obviously more than an ontological problem for Mr Jeremy, as it went to the heart of his defence. Why should the jury believe what Field said in court, when he openly admitted that he had spent most of his life deceiving people? Why should they now believe that he was telling the truth when, for whatever reason, Field had revealed that throughout his life he had been a consistent liar? I rather got the impression that what Field was doing in court, as he had done throughout his whole life, was creating his own reality. That's one kind of truth.

What Field says on Day 23 is interesting from two other perspectives: first, it confirms that he and Peter had often used what they had written as a 'medium' to communicate with each other; and, second, the idea that 'most of my pleasures have been privately held' is, it would seem, the basis that exculpates both his brother and Martyn Smith. In other words, he had not shared with them the details about what he was doing in Maids Moreton, and therefore they were not privy to the frauds or the burglaries. Of course, the prosecution believed they had evidence which indicated they were aware of what was happening, but this evidence did not persuade the jury.

One question here is why would Field be prepared to fall on his sword, if that is indeed what he did, rather than try to implicate others? This might take us back to the P-SCAN and the fact that Field scored lowest on the lifestyle facet: he had held down a job; graduated from school and university; and he did not live life in the fast lane. I suggested that this was probably down to the influence of his parents, and their insistence on living life by the values they believed to be important.

The idea that Field and Peter communicated with each other through their writing is at the heart of the argument in this book, and so I was pleased to hear Field confirm this in the witness box. What they wrote was a 'medium' to discuss ideas; share secrets; and tease and please each other. Of course, in court Mr Jeremy wants Field to use this reality to explain to the jury that his poems – his 'rap battles' – were just 'a bit of sport' and that he took no pleasure in 'positive types of writing'. He also wanted to harness this to the fact that they had had a 'long-running literary debate' about what was most important in literature. Peter had enjoyed the moral substance and meaning of the text, whereas Field had preferred the language and the 'wordplay'. As Mr Jeremy put it, and which Field accepted, his preference was for 'style over substance'. This takes us back to Paul Muldoon, ergodicity and Field's

MA dissertation. Field likes playing word games and sees himself as an equal contributor to the creation of any text. Was what he said in court not also a contribution to another and different form of wordplay and text? In other words, to present a competing narrative of why he was on trial and a defence to what was alleged by the prosecution? However, in the same way that Professor Tim Kendall, who had marked Field's dissertation, suggested to me that Field 'wanted the examiners to award a mark: on what basis? It is after all our prerogative to find these games unnecessary, inappropriate, unenlightening, [and] frivolous', he was now expecting the court to do the same, not by passing his dissertation but by finding him not guilty.

But the jury would subsequently find his testimony inappropriate and unenlightening, and so they came to a different verdict.

I was fascinated by Field's acceptance that his was a preference for 'style over substance'. This phrase is often used to describe psychopathy. The psychopath at first appears attractive: they say things and behave in ways that we would never dream of doing and so we are initially drawn to them, but in the end it is possible to see through all of this style to their lack of depth; they have no genuine core to who they are, and so find it easy to live only in the moment. They live in the moment because they have no sense of the future. They rarely plan or think ahead. They dazzle and astonish, but be warned: what glitters is base metal, not gold.

I have already discussed several of the issues in relation to the closing addresses by the prosecution and the defence to the jury, especially with regard to what is the truth. Here I simply want to concentrate on Mr Jeremy's defence and his use of two statements: first, 'I regard it as a privilege to represent Ben Field'; and, second, 'They were two odd people united in their oddness.' The first seems to have more behind it than the legal truism that everyone deserves a fair trial, although Mr Jeremy would go on to say that Field was 'somebody's son, somebody's brother', which perhaps does hint at this truism, which is the basis of our justice system. However, what he is also doing is implying that Field has been an especially interesting client, and so it has been a pleasure and honour – both synonyms for privilege – to have represented him. He is trying to get the jury to look at Field in this way: as a young man who is academically bright and extremely talented; to look at him as someone who simply could not kill.

The second statement has, for me, echoes of what Mr Jeremy said in his summary at the trial of Danilo Restivo, who he defended in 2011: that he was 'a deeply unattractive oddity'. I would happily accept that description for both Restivo and Field – after all, they had both committed murder – but it seems to me to be going too far to try to also apply that description to Peter. What was odd about him? The fact that he was single, elderly, an academic, Christian, an author, or that he was gay? Of course, this statement might have been used to plant a seed in the jury's thinking that Peter and Field were an 'odd couple', which in itself would explain Field's often curious behaviour. However, for me, it plays on stereotypes of what is socially acceptable and what is not; stereotypes which are rooted in popular conventions about what can be viewed as 'normal' and acceptable, and with what might be regarded as 'odd'. It is also rather insensitive.

Allied to all of this was Mr Jeremy's proposition – his defence – that Peter 'could have died from taking his normal dose of flurazepam and drinking "too much"'. This would also become part of the basis of an appeal against conviction in 2020.

In the end the jury rejected all of this and found Field guilty of murder.

*

In his sentencing remarks, the Honourable Mr Justice Sweeney stated that Peter's murder had been 'for gain' and that there were a number of aggravating features about Field's crime which included: planning and premeditation; the mental and physical suffering that he had inflicted on Peter; and an abuse of his position of trust. All of this meant that the minimum term for the murder would be thirty-two years, and for the other charges related to the frauds and burglaries he would receive a further four and half years, although this would be rounded down to four years. The total minimum term that Field would have to serve would therefore be thirty-six years, before he could then become eligible for parole. The judge also described Field as 'cruel', and said 'I have no doubt that you are a dangerous offender'. However, I want to give the last word here on all of this to Mark Glover, my Roundhead in Operation Naseby rather than one of the Oxford Cavaliers, and I have coupled some of his formal comments in the TVP's press statement with things that he said to me during our interview:

This was unlike any investigation I have previously worked on in my thirty-one years of police service. Ben has showed no remorse for what he has done and I am convinced that he is unable to show human empathy. Ben's arrogance led him to believe that he could literally get away with murder. I am convinced that had he not been stopped, he would have posed an ongoing danger to society.

Ben Field is all about Ben Field. That's how I would sum it all up.

Summing things up offers a form of closure and of moving forward; of putting the past behind us. That seems fair enough for the police. However, it seems to me that there are things that need to be acknowledged about what had happened and then lessons learned from this case by a number of individuals and institutions about how they should conduct themselves in the future.

Before his arrest for murder, Field was just five days away from going forward to the Bishop's Advisory Panel – the final stage of the discernment process before being accepted for ordination training – and he was also teaching on undergraduate seminars at UB. His conviction and imprisonment might have provided one form of closure, but what guarantees do we have that the Church and the university could not still become susceptible to another Ben Field in the years to come? At the very least, the university needs to be far more open about its 'poster boy' and how he came to be in a relationship with not one but two of his supervisors, and why it chose to publish his MA dissertation. To make an obvious point, it simply isn't good pedagogic practice to start a relationship with a student that you are supposed to be supervising; frankly, at the very least, it is an abuse of power. Addressing these matters might be painful and involve both institutional and interpersonal issues, but I'd like to think that UB's internal procedures are robust enough to be able to look far more critically – and publicly – at what had gone on within the university after Ben Field started his degree in English literature.

And what is true for UB is perhaps even more important for the Church.

We need to look backwards, so that we can also look to the future.

Lest we forget.

CHAPTER TEN

Reading the Lesson

> "'Why I was in a choir once," the boy confided
> and suddenly he began to sing softly in his spoilt
> boy's voice: *"Agnus dei qui tollis peccata mundi
> dona nobis pacem"'*
>
> PINKIE BROWN in Graham Greene,
> *Brighton Rock*

I like walking – it's one of the ways I keep my weight down – and regularly average, through rain and shine, about fifty miles a week. One day in 2019 I decided to deviate from one of my regular routes to find Stowe Parish Church. It is also sometimes known as St Mary's or, to give it its full title, the Church of the Assumption of the Blessed Virgin Mary, and it is now all that remains of the medieval village of Stowe. The church is more than eight hundred years old. The earliest printed records about the church date from the thirteenth century, and there is an ancient yew tree just outside the churchyard, which also appears to date from this time. Lancelot 'Capability' Brown, who spent much of the early part of his career as a landscape architect at Stowe, was married in the church in 1744, and all four of his children were baptised there too. Brown designed over 170 parks and gardens and was nicknamed Capability because he would tell his prospective clients that their properties had the 'capability' for improvement.

I slowly pushed open the inevitably squeaky wooden door and, once my eyes had become accustomed to the gloomy interior, I looked around. I noted a few ornate tombs, six bells in the tower, an effigy, a crypt, some crude memorial brass, and a large memorial window that allowed some natural light to shine inside.

These scant, historical highlights might make Stowe Parish Church appear rather more quaint or romantic than it actually is because, while not wishing to be unkind, it is a rather ugly hodgepodge of a place; it has a failing roof, and dark, damp-threatened walls. When I visited, I could hardly wait to get out and back to my walk in the fresh air and daylight.

The church dutifully plays the role of an ugly duckling to the beautiful swan of the Arcadian dream of Stowe House and its landscaped gardens. Frankly, it stands out like a sore thumb and perhaps that was the point. Lord Cobham, who redesigned the existing Stowe House and its gardens in the first half of the eighteenth century, had no time for religion – those were his Enlightenment values – and so he didn't want a medieval church spoiling the classical landscape he was creating. As a result, he hid the old church behind some trees, and didn't bother too much about it as long as it couldn't be seen. It's a wonder it survived at all.

Of course it did survive, and is today an active parish church that covers a wide geographic area. Peter and his mother Annie, who died in 2002 and was buried in the churchyard, were members of the congregation. Peter clearly found his faith a comfort and he sometimes acted as a lay preacher. After his death an anonymous short tribute to him appeared in the parish magazine for January–February 2020 (and therefore it couldn't have been written by Field, who was by that time in HMP Durham), alongside which is reproduced his graduation photograph from Cambridge University. This short tribute is in the form of a villanelle and its metre con-sciously copies, we are told, 'a poem he must have often taught, Dylan Thomas' "Do not go gentle into that good night"':

In school crusadingly he stood for right,
Gaining his points a dry, effective way,
Mighty in word power, though in stature slight.

Swift to reject the tawdry and the trite,
He aimed for higher things to win the day –
A school where poetry and plays excite.

A swift detention was the slacker's plight.
A beta minus could cause dismay!
So pupils learnt to work, then soared in flight.

The Bible was his solace and delight.
He trod a thoughtful path, the Word his stay,
The Lord in constancy met day and night.

His depth of knowledge sometimes could affright!
Those Bible quizzes might turn vicars grey.
Begowned, he dazzled from the pulpit's height:

All modern foibles with a smile he'd smite,
All modern vices with a sigh he'd flay –
Yet 'chivarous' and 'meeke', like Chaucer's Knight.

His prayers, like sparks, would all his plans ignite.
To share his prayers, wherever, was his way,
The Bull & Butcher's garden once the site!

We have encountered some of these tropes before: Peter's small stature did not prevent him from getting his point across; reference is made to his desire to allow his pupils to fulfil their potential; as is the love that he had for literature – or, as expressed in this case, 'poetry and plays'. However, a number of new elements are introduced too, and these concern Peter's faith. So, we are told: the Bible was his solace, and he had a great deal of biblical knowledge; the Lord was his constancy; he was an excellent preacher – his prayers were like 'sparks'; and he disliked modern vices and foibles. The Bull & Butcher in the final line is a reference to a local pub, in the nearby village of Akeley.

I have no doubt that Peter was sincere in his faith, and that it brought him comfort. Nor am I questioning the sincerity of this short tribute. However, his faith should also make us pause to consider some difficulties, for it is quite clear that he did not 'flay' or 'smite' all 'modern foibles and vices' at all; he would eventually set up home with a young man in a same-sex relationship. How did this sit with Peter's faith, his sense of himself and the image that he wanted to project to others, and what problems might this have posed for him within the congregation of Stowe Parish Church? As some might have seen it, Peter was actively embracing a moral failing as a fundamental and essential part of who he was, within a religious and institutional culture that has never been welcoming of homosexuality, and has routinely seen gay sex as a sin.

The current formal position of the Church of England (CoE) on these matters can be dated back to a Statement by the House of Bishops made in December 1991, called *Issues in Human Sexuality*. This made it clear that 'heterosexuality and homosexuality are not equally congruous with the observed order of creation or with the insights of revelation as the Church engages with these in the light of her pastoral ministry'. Gay people of faith, in other words, could not claim the same rights as those who were straight, and 'Christian homophiles [*sic*]' were advised that 'they must follow to fulfil [their] calling to witness to God's general will for human sexuality by a life of abstinence', or 'self-denial'. As recently as 2019, in a House of Bishops Statement on civil partnerships, the CoE made it clear that sex only belongs within heterosexual marriage and that sex within gay, or straight, civil partnerships 'falls short of God's purpose for human beings'. The CoE still does not permit same-sex marriage. The pastoral guidance that accompanied this statement is, we are advised, summarised in *The Book of Common Prayer*, where the marriage service lists the causes for which matrimony was ordained: 'for the procreation of children', 'for a remedy against sin' and 'for the mutual society, help and comfort that the one ought to have of the other'.

There is of course a great deal of opposition to the position held by the CoE on these matters. We have already met Fr Andrew Foreshew-Cain, described in the *Guardian* as 'a rebel priest', who believes that the CoE's position is 'abusive' and implies that 'God will only accept you if you don't have sex; that is if you don't want what everybody wants, which is to be loved by somebody and to love them on their terms'. Fr Andrew, who married his partner Stephen in 2014, is now the college chaplain at Lady Margaret Hall in Oxford, but was previously the vicar at St Mary's, West Hampstead. It was there that he performed the betrothal ceremony between Peter and Field, and he was also described in the *Church Times* as having been Peter's 'spiritual director for several years'.

It is clear that Peter's faith was far from unproblematic, to the extent that his spiritual director was a rebel priest. The idea therefore that he smote and flayed all modern foibles and vices is pretty wide of the mark, given that he was clearly struggling to reconcile his sexuality with the formal position of the CoE. This reality also helps us to begin to frame another way to understand the very public protestations that the relationship between Peter and Field was platonic, rather than sexual, especially as Field was also attempting to go through the process of ordination within the CoE.

Of course, all of this poses a number of other questions. Why did Peter need a spiritual director, and when did that relationship begin? Why was the betrothal ceremony in London, rather than at Stowe Parish Church, which had been so important to him? More broadly, these questions begin to force us – no matter how painful it is – to consider whether what happened to Peter was only possible because a motivated offender found an institutional context that allowed him to become a murderer.

When I spoke with Fr Andrew, he answered my question about why Peter and Field had had their betrothal ceremony in London quite simply. 'Peter wasn't out at Stowe Church, or at the school,' he said. 'He'd had a colleague at Manchester Grammar School who was sacked after he came out as gay, and Peter learned from that experience. He might have fantasised about young, intelligent men at Stowe, but he learned never to do or say anything about those fantasies.' But then why bother to worship at Stowe Parish Church, which Fr Andrew described to me as being 'a charismatic church and so everything about Peter's sexuality was against what they believed in'? Fr Andrew suggested that Peter could have intelligent conversations there about matters of faith, which was important to him, and even if some of the congregation might have guessed that he was gay, 'it had that eighties attitude of "don't ask, don't tell".' Silence, in other words, or at least knowing but choosing not to know, became a context to understand this murder; to have challenged the relationship that had developed between Peter and Field would, in other words, have involved acknowledging that the pair were actually in a relationship which was seen as sinful and therefore against the Church's teachings. It later struck me that Peter's mother had worshipped at Stowe Parish Church too, which must also have created a familial bond to the place.

As for my other questions, Peter had started to see Fr Andrew as a spiritual director after arranging to visit a psychotherapist in West Hampstead. 'It was soon clear,' Fr Andrew stated, 'that Peter didn't need psychotherapy, but just needed to talk to another Christian who was gay to discuss his sexuality. St Mary's is next door to where the psychotherapist used to practise and that's how Peter started to come and see me.' He saw Peter for just over two years. 'Ben was the type of person that Peter fantasised about: a younger man who was well read,' Fr Andrew said. He went further, and was clearly still infuriated by what had happened to Peter. He said, 'I blame the Church of England for Peter's death. They are so screwed up about sexuality and Christianity that it creates situations that can be exploited by someone like Ben. I'm very angry at the Church and no matter what internal review they've completed, they need to think about what is central in this case – sexuality and the Church's views about being gay.'

There are a number of ways to process all of this information, and they make the narratives about Peter's murder much less certain, or clear-cut. Offenders typically commit crimes in situations which they can exploit because there are no formal, or informal, guardians to prevent those crimes from occurring. So, first, we need to think about how the CoE's attitudes towards sexuality actively created the circumstances that Field could exploit to his own advantage. In doing so we must both guard against a simple reclaiming of Peter as a member of the congregation at Stowe Parish Church after his death, and a responsibilising of his murderer. Second, as in my earlier discussions of splitting, it becomes clear that Peter no longer wanted to deny the reality of his sexuality, although this had clearly at one stage troubled him sufficiently to seek out a psychotherapist. That, in turn, had led to spiritual guidance from a rebel priest – a priest, moreover, who was openly gay and had married his partner. Fr Andrew was a model of what was possible in West Hampstead, although could this model be applied equally in Buckingham and Maids Moreton?

Clearly not, and so Stowe Parish Church chose to manage what was happening in a similar way to the wider community: it didn't ask too many questions, pry too deeply, and simply got on with its own life as it always had done. Don't ask; don't tell. We know, but we choose not to know and so we don't know. So it included, without really ever accepting, other than on its own terms.

It does seem obvious to me that, at the end of his life, Peter was trying to repair the 'spilt' and was no longer willing, as a gay Christian, simply to romanticise his options and imagine himself eloping – like the Owl and the Pussy-cat on a beautiful pea-green boat. In fact we know from Field's writings that Edward Lear's 'nonsense poem', published in 1871, was very important to him, and it is difficult to ignore that the subtext of the inter-species love that it celebrates mirrors metaphorically his relationship with Peter. As for Peter, I'd like to think that he had at last answered the question that he had set at the heart of his narrative in *Between Boy and Man* of whether sensual pleasures and altruism were incompatible.

The Church's inability to accept Peter's sexuality is one of the major issues in this case, and the broader context in which to view his murder. However, so too is the power that Field was able to yield inside Stowe Parish Church, with the awful possibility that he might have been on the brink of even greater powers within the diocese. Did he really have any religious conviction?

214

From the start of 2020 I had been having regular discussions about Field and Peter's murder with a friend who works as a forensic psychologist. Over one of our cups of coffee at my university in Birmingham I asked my friend, who prefers to remain anonymous and so I will only refer to him as 'FP', about Field and religion. Here are some snatches of that conversation that I feel offers us some insight into this question about Field and his faith:

DW: Do you think that Field's religious claims
were sincere?

FP: No. That was all part of the game that he was
playing. He's just using religion to gain access to
elderly people. Of course he says the right things –
he's a good actor. And, because he's a good actor,
he plays the role well. But we both know that he's a
psychopath: he just wants their money …

DW: … but there's more than that too – he wants more
than their money; he wasn't even particularly flash.

FP: I agree. He wants power. That's what gives him
satisfaction.

DW: He targeted two teachers and his father is a
minister. There must be something going on here;
this seems to be about subverting power.

FP: Yes. It strikes me, though, that his father's ministry
also simply gives him the language, the tone and
the behaviour about how to conduct himself in that
religious world. That's why he is so good at carrying
this off – he already knows how to behave in that
culture and so he will appear to be sincere. I'm not

certain about the teacher aspect to what he does, but if you think about it, in traditional societies, they had a position of authority too: the teacher, the priest; Church and school.

DW: He pretty nearly perfected this act. He was just days away from possibly being accepted onto ordination training. Do you think that he would have stopped killing?

FP: I know, that's frightening. Just imagine if he had become a priest. No. He would have continued to kill until he was caught – you know that better than I do! He'd have killed as many as he could have got away with killing.

DW: Of course, that's about power too.

This discussion opens up territory that really does need to be explored, beyond the sincerity or otherwise of Field's religious views. His supposed religious understanding was, at best, a pick-and-mix spirituality that suited his own needs, and which of course accommodated murder. However, the idea that Field had used his father's ministry to learn how to conduct himself within the religious world is clearly something that needs to be taken seriously. Above all, we need to understand how he was able to be just days away from attending a Bishop's Advisory Panel – the final stage of the discernment process before being accepted onto ordination training.

The Church was very close to recruiting a killer and someone whom many, including Mark Glover, the SIO who investigated the case, believe would have killed again and again until he was stopped.

Field's motivation to go through the discernment process and seek ordination wasn't the result of his faith, or about his calling and love of God; he was merely using religion to gain access to people that he wanted to target, and deploying his knowledge of how to behave in this world to mask his true intentions. His religiosity was, like most of his life, inauthentic. He was mirroring how to be religious, in the same way that Tom Ripley mirrored the mannerisms of Dickie Greenleaf, or the monster mirrored behaviours in *Frankenstein*. He had learned all the right words to say and when to say them; how to use the right tone and pitch of his voice; and how his words could provide hope and comfort to those in distress. But it was all a game, a sham, simply a ruse to gain access to elderly people who might be 'useful' to him, rather than providing them with comfort in their moment of need. How would he have taunted them when they lay close to death?

If he had got that far, Field would not have been the first minister to murder members of his own congregation, or even the first murderer to become a minister. The Scottish literary critic Stuart Kelly, for example, describes the case of James Nelson, who murdered his mother in Glasgow in 1969 in a fit of rage and was sentenced to life imprisonment. Fifteen years later, in 1984, after he had been released on parole and had studied theology at St Andrews, he applied to become a minister in the Church of Scotland. His application split the General Assembly of the Church but, after a three-hour debate, they voted in his favour and Nelson became the first convicted killer to be ordained into a Christian Church. Until his death in 2005 he was the minister of Chapelhall and Calderbank in Lanarkshire which, as Kelly describes, was 'a brisk twenty-minute walk from where he had killed his mother'. In a strange twist of fate, Nelson appeared on the same episode of *After Dark* as Patricia Highsmith in 1988.

We might see Nelson as a 'bad man who became good' but there are many 'good men and some women who have gone bad'. The idea that men and women of the cloth can kill is now so widely accepted that the true crime TV channel CBS Reality has a documentary series called *Killer Clergy*, and there are various top-ten lists of murderous priests, pastors and nuns on the internet. However Field, it seems to me, would have been in a new category altogether: a bad man who was using good to continue to be bad. Not so much an angel at church and a devil at home, but always a devil and everywhere.

As a modest balance to the 'good men gone bad' trope, we should also note that several murderers have deliberately targeted priests. The case of the serial killer Patrick Mackay is of double interest here for not only was he a gerontophile, who repeatedly attacked and killed elderly women, but his final victim was Father Anthony Crean, who he murdered in March 1975 in the most horrific manner, despite the fact that the sixty-four-year-old priest had once befriended him. Not content with stabbing Fr Crean in the head, Mackay also used an axe to hack at the poor man's skull.

Mackay, who was sometimes known in the press as 'the devil's disciple', is still in prison and his parole hearing scheduled for 2020 was delayed as he is suspected of other historic murders which are currently being (re)investigated. We do not know for certain which cases the police are considering, but it would hardly come as a surprise if these involved elderly women. Mackay thought that the elderly were easy targets because they were vulnerable and defenceless. His first victim was Isabella Griffiths, who he killed in February 1974 in Chelsea, although he was not apprehended at that time. He was sentenced to four months' imprisonment for theft in July 1974 and, while he was serving his sentence in HMP Wormwood Scrubs, hatched a plan a plan to rob and kill other elderly women. On his release from prison, he began what the press later called a 'reign of terror' during the winter of 1974–5 that saw him attack eighty-year-old Jane Comfort, an actress who was appearing in Agatha Christie's *The Mousetrap*, Lady Belcher and two other women, although he did not kill them. In January 1975 he targeted a hostel to rob in Vandon Street in Westminster that specifically catered for elderly women, although robbing his victims clearly wasn't enough – he wanted to go further. In March 1975 he strangled eighty-nine-year-old Adele Price in Knightsbridge, before travelling down to Gravesend, where he would kill Fr Crean.

There may have been a sexual motive for his targeting of elderly female victims, as his behaviour seemed to echo a pattern of attacking his mother in his youth – there was a suggestion that he was trying to 'take the place' of his dead father – and these beatings became so severe that his mother had to have him removed from the family home on eighteen different occasions. However, the reasons why any offender chooses to act in a certain way can accommodate a range of benefits and emotions that easily transcend a simple analysis and might include the immediate instrumental gains that can come with robbery, for example, as well as more expressive psychological rewards. To complicate matters further, an offender might start out with one goal in mind but realise that his offending offers him other opportunities too. So, for example, he might want to rob and steal, but in doing so he might begin to enjoy the feelings of power that this engenders, to the extent that stealing becomes secondary to what he wants to achieve. When this happens we often see offenders escalate their offending, both in terms of the frequency they offend, and in terms of the types of crimes that they commit.

Mackay had what might be called the classic background of a serial killer. His father was a violent alcoholic who regularly beat him, and he found some solace in torturing small animals and bullying other children. He was a loner, attended school only intermittently and got into trouble with the police for various offences when he was a child. By the age of fifteen he was already being described by one psychiatrist who interviewed him as 'a cold psychopathic killer', and he would eventually be detained under the Mental Health Act.

Of course, all of this is in marked contrast to Field's background, where a loving family had ensured that he attended school and would go on to university. Even so, there are similarities between the two. The escalation which we see in Mackay's offending can also be inferred from Field's list of other people that he might target after he had killed Peter. So too the sense that both might have sought expressive psychological rewards from their offending, which were more important to them than what might be gained instrumentally, helps to explain why Field didn't seem to live his life in the 'fast lane' and creates a link between the two murderers, despite their differing backgrounds.

What is different is that Mackay never expressed any religious feelings – he was obsessed with Nazism, and only seems to have targeted Father Crean out of spite. So how should we make sense of Field's use of religion? Let's turn again to literature, for there is one final, murderous literary character that Field had studied at university who claimed that he had faith too, and who also seems to have influenced how the mechanics of Peter's murder were shaped.

*

The final fictional character I want to examine, and who Field studied at UB in a module about 'modernist writing' taught by Peter, is Pinkie Brown, the teenage murderer in Graham Greene's *Brighton Rock*. Pinkie used murder to solve his problems too, and also religion to ensure the silence of his future wife Rose.

Brighton Rock was Graham Greene's ninth novel, and was published in 1938. Greene was a fan of both Henry James and, later, of Patricia Highsmith too, and *Brighton Rock* can be viewed as his first overtly Catholic novel. Like the other characters that would come to inhabit 'Greeneland' in his later novels, such as *The Power and the Glory* and *The Heart of the Matter*, the men in *Brighton Rock* are flawed, their beliefs are sorely tested, and God, if he exists, in Greene's novels is omnipresent but mysterious, contentious and hidden. The main theme of the novel is the attempt to reconcile faith with the harsh realities of life. The Brighton of *Brighton Rock* was one of crushing poverty, razor gangs and villains, rather than the pier, day-trippers and ice creams. Throughout the narrative there is a pervading sense of impending disaster, mortal sin and a life-and-death struggle between good and evil.

The action in *Brighton Rock* can be viewed as the sequel to Greene's 1936 novel *A Gun for Sale*, which concerned the

221

death of a gang leader called Kite. Kite had been murdered by the rival Colleoni gang, after he had been betrayed partly through information provided by a reporter called Charles 'Fred' Hale, and at the start of *Brighton Rock* we discover Hale back in Brighton.

Pinkie Brown had been Kite's lieutenant, but he is now the new gang leader and so responsible for the other gang members – Spicer, Cubitt and Darrow. He wants to avenge Kite by killing Hale. Pinkie is only seventeen years old, terrified of sex – he is still a virgin, a misogynist and totally psychopathic. We glimpse this latter aspect of his personality when Pinkie is described as being unable to 'see through other people's eyes, or feel with their nerves'. Pinkie therefore has no qualms about killing, and not only does he and his gang murder Hale but he goes on to kill others too. As he explains, 'When people do one murder, I've read they sometimes have to do another – to tidy up.' More graphically, Pinkie 'trailed the clouds of his own glory after him; Hell lay about him in his infancy. He was ready for more deaths.' Pinkie used murder as a solution to his problems and, wherever he went, he carried with him a bottle of vitriol – sulphuric acid.

Quite apart from Pinkie's 'soured virginity' or, as it is sometimes termed, his 'bitter virginity' (the result of his misogyny, and having had to watch his parents have sex when he was younger), he is characterised as having been brought up in the Catholic faith. One weakness in the plot is the ability of the uneducated, youthful Pinkie to drop into perfect Latin whenever he chooses. However, faith for Pinkie is all about fire and brimstone; Hell and damnation; his God is one who punishes and damns, rather than forgives. He uses his faith to seduce

Rose, who was the café waitress who served Hale on the day he was murdered. Pinkie fears that she might be able to provide valuable information to the police that will incriminate him and his gang and so he sets out to seduce Rose to ensure her silence. Rose is also a Catholic, although her faith is in a God that redeems and forgives; she concentrates on Heaven, rather than Hell.

On the day of his death, Hale by chance briefly becomes friendly with larger-than-life, non-religious Ida Arnold and it is she who will in turn become an ambiguous detective figure in the novel, as it is Ida who wants to get to the bottom of why Hale died. She doesn't accept the post-mortem report that he had died of a heart attack, even if the police try to dissuade her from pursuing the matter.

As J. M. Coetzee notes in his introduction to the Penguin Classics edition, *Brighton Rock* is a novel without a hero, only characters who are less, or more objectionable. If there is a force for good it is Ida Arnold, an unconventional private detective, but she fails to understand why Rose doesn't want to leave Pinkie; Rose doesn't want to be 'saved' by Ida because she already believes she has been saved by Pinkie. She knows all about the murders he has committed, but she loves him unconditionally; her faith in him never wavers. As Coetzee puts it, 'The story of Pinkie and Rose is the story, on Pinkie's side, of a struggle to bar the entry of love into his heart, on Rose's of dogged persistence in love in the face of all prudence.' And then, perhaps capturing something of Peter and Field's own betrothal ceremony, Coetzee argues that 'To preclude Rose from testifying against him if he is ever brought to trial, Pinkie marries her in a civil ceremony that both know to be a sin against the Holy Ghost.' In other words, the ceremony guaranteed her silence.

Pinkie, the 'soured' virgin, discovers that he does in fact quite like sex: it makes him feel powerful. After their marriage Pinkie and Rose wander around Brighton and she begs him to record something on a gramophone record to commemorate the occasion. Rose presumes that Pinkie will record something suitably romantic, but in fact it is a hateful rant about how she has trapped him. However, as they do not have a gramophone player, and he hopes to convince her to kill herself, he presumes that she will never hear what he has said.

The climax of the action takes place in Peacehaven, where Pinkie is going to get Rose to kill herself in a suicide pact he has no intention of honouring. Just in time, Ida arrives with the police and Pinkie kills himself. Rose is left in deep mourning for Pinkie, and goes to confession. The priest, rather than damning her, tells her that God's mercy is infinite. Suitably relieved, she leaves the church in search of a shop where she can play the gramophone record and listen to what she believes will be a sweet message of love that Pinkie has left for her. We do not know if her faith will survive the horrible message that he has recorded, and nor do we know if Pinkie will find himself in Heaven, or in Hell.

Even these bare outlines of *Brighton Rock* offer a rather illuminating insight into the relationship between Field and Peter, with the characters and motives of both Rose and Pinkie suggesting something about life in Maids Moreton in 2015, as well as in the fictional Brighton of the 1930s.

The soured and bitter virginity that Pinkie has trapped himself in and can find no way out of seems to replicate itself in Peter's circumstances. I was particularly struck by Coetzee's observation about the dynamic within the fictional relationship: on Pinkie's side, an attempt 'to bar the entry of love into his heart', and the 'dogged persistence in love in the face of all prudence' on Rose's. These extremes suggest something of Peter's individual circumstances and the personal struggle that he had faced throughout his life. Should he be his true self as a gay man, or a divided self, who denied himself the comforts of love and had to perpetually mask his libidinal impulses? Pinkie's psychopathy was so prevalent that he could not 'see through other people's eyes, or feel with their nerves' and this corresponded with scores that I gave to Field on the P-SCAN. Of course, like Pinkie, Field would also use murder as a means to deal with his problems. Marriage had ensured Rose's silence and her commitment to Pinkie – is that how we should also interpret Peter's failure to leave Field after they had gone through their betrothal ceremony?

We do not discover what Rose made of the message Pinkie recorded to her on their wedding day; her reaction is left to our imagination. Nor do we know how poor Peter might have reacted to Field telling him as he lay dying, 'I hated you all along' – taunting him with vitriol and malice. Where had the inspiration for this terrible denouement come from? I have no doubt from Pinkie Brown in *Brighton Rock*.

More's the pity that Peter had no Ida Arnold to doggedly challenge the first post-mortem, although I did try.

Pinkie's character is of even greater relevance to how to understand Field because of the use that he makes of religion. We should also remember that this was a book that Field studied as part of his degree and which had been taught by Peter. Religion was Pinkie's calling card, which served to create a common interest with Rose. It was something that Pinkie claimed they shared from their past, and which he could use to unite them still further when it suited his needs. Theirs is an unconventional relationship, but their shared faith affords Greene the opportunity to infuse the narrative with questions about good and evil, Heaven and Hell, redemption and damnation.

However, at a much more immediate level, religion created a bond of trust between Rose and Pinkie. In one sense, he would even become her God; she certainly showed unwavering faith in him, despite all the evidence that suggested that this was foolhardy and misplaced.

Rose was dazzled by Pinkie, in much the same way that Peter – and a number of others – were dazzled by Field.

*

In August 2019, in the wake of Field's trial, the Venerable Guy Elsmore, Archdeacon of Buckingham, released a statement on behalf of the diocese, remembering in their prayers the friends and family of Peter and 'those who worship at Stowe Parish Church, where Peter worshipped, and the community of Maids Moreton where he lived'. He took comfort from the fact that, at times like this, Christian communities come into their own, although he also thought that the case had things to teach the Church about safeguarding, and that there would be a 'lessons learned' review. However, he emphasised that:

This has been an extraordinary and unusual case. No one who came into contact with Ben Field was not manipulated by him. He made a pretence of being a committed

Christian and gained the confidence of the people of Stowe Parish Church and then, to quote his own words, *'I'm gonna become a vicar ... just because I can outmanoeuvre the church.'* His arrest put an end to this pretence.

The Archdeacon's statement was followed by 'Information for journalists' which consisted of five bullet points. Three of these were the facts that Field had joined Stowe Parish Church in 2013; he had become secretary to the Parochial Church Council in September 2014; and he had been confirmed at Stowe in November 2015. The two other bullet points stated: 'Was Ben Field a "trainee vicar"? No – Field was never considered for ordination training'; and 'Ben Field became a "deputy warden" at the church in September 2014. The role of deputy warden is not a formal office in the Church of England and has no legal definition.'

I can appreciate a desire for the Diocese of Oxford to want to move on, to put what had happened at Stowe Parish Church behind them. However, this statement simply won't do. The fact of Field's arrest – and then conviction – might have put an end to his personal 'pretence', but it is surely only the beginning, and not the end, of needing to think through things carefully at an institutional level. Unless the Church is prepared to be honest about how all of this could have happened, there will always be a danger of more Ben Fields in the future, or indeed working in the clergy now.

I am reminded here of what Nassim Nicholas Taleb wrote about in *The Black Swan: The Impact of the Highly Improbable.* For Taleb, the world is dominated by the extreme and improbable, and yet we spend far too much time discussing what is known about 'normal' events and behaviour, so 'exceptional' events are 'swept under the rug'. He calls these improbable and exceptional events which can have a massive impact on society 'black swans', and suggests that their existence exposes, among other things, the limitations of learning from experience. Taleb describes a black swan event as being extremely unpredictable and as an outlier – it exists beyond the expected ways of behaving.

Taleb says we need to adjust our thinking to the existence of black swans. He argues that we need to study the exceptional event in order to understand events which are common. A failure to understand the black swan event, he warns, can have disastrous consequences and carry a devastating cumulative effect.

If we applied the idea of the black swan to the Diocese's thinking, it becomes clear that they are not trying to learn from what was clearly something exceptional; they are instead, to use Taleb's phrase, wanting to sweep Field 'under the rug'. It isn't good enough, for example, to state that 'Field was never considered for ordination training'.

A straightforward look at the facts indicates that he was.

Field had his first formal pre-ordination meeting with the Reverend Caroline Windley, the Diocesan Director of Ordinands, in April 2016. It was the Reverend Windley's job to meet with prospective priests 'over an extended period of time, to confirm that your calling is informed and realistic'. Then, 'when the Director of Ordinands is satisfied that you may indeed be called to ordained ministry (s)he will arrange for the Bishop to send you to a Bishop's Advisory Panel (a BAP) where your calling will be tested by people skilled in the discernment process'. The Reverend Windley formally met with Field eight times between April and November 2016, and, prior to that, he had been seeing a vocations adviser. In January 2017 the psychotherapist Stephen Bushell had raised 'serious concerns' (and I have debated whether or not he offered a clinical diagnosis of psychopathy) about Field to Reverend Windley, but despite these concerns he was still going to go forward to the BAP. It was his arrest on the charge of murder that put a stop to Field's 'pretence', not the Church of England's discernment process.

Nor should we accept the simple disowning of Field's role at Stowe Parish Church that is evident within the second bullet point in the 'Information for journalists'. It is quite true that the role of deputy warden is an informal one and so has no legal standing within the Church of England. However, he was secretary to the PCC, and being elected by other members of the congregation to the role of 'deputy' warden implies how embedded at the church he had become within a very short period of time. I also interviewed two parishioners who assured me that Field had even administered the sacraments of Holy Communion.

Even so, 'RS', writing in the September 2019 edition of the parish magazine, wanted to distance Stowe Parish Church from Field in much the same way that the Diocese of Oxford was distancing itself from the newly convicted killer. He stated that Field was not a church warden – 'the accused bore no such title' – and 'in Peter's memory', he wanted to pay tribute to his 'long-standing, respected and devout' membership of the Church. RS makes no mention of Peter's sexuality and, despite his protestations, it is hard not to conclude that Stowe

Parish Church, and the Diocese of Oxford more generally, had been dazzled by Field as completely as Peter had been, and in much the same way that Pinkie dazzled Rose. Field was a young, educated man who wanted to become a priest, and at a time when church-going has increasingly become something for those over the age of sixty; he was a company director; and he was a published author who took seminars for undergraduates at the local university.

What was not to like?

Well, he was a psychopath, and our best estimate is that one person in every one hundred of the general population will also be a psychopath. How is the Church going to weed out that 1 per cent during their discernment process, and, more worryingly, how are we to know that there aren't already other psychopaths already ministering within a parish?

Just as well the Diocese was going to consider the lessons that it needed to learn.

*

I first heard of the 'lessons learned' review in August 2019 as a result of Elsmore's statement, although at that stage I did not know who would undertake such a review, when it would be completed, or if it would then be published. I gave things a few months, but from January 2020 I was constantly contacting Steven Buckley, who handles press relations at the Diocese of Oxford, to find out when the review was going to be finished, and whether it would be made public. Steven explained that he thought that it would be published and, at least initially, he seemed to be open to a dialogue with me about events in Maids Moreton. As the months wore on, and certainly by May 2020, Steven seemed less happy to hear from me and, when I persisted in asking when the review was to be published, he merely replied 'imminently'.

Every day I would check the Diocese of Oxford website to see if the learning review had been published, so I got to know all about the workings of the diocese. On their news feed in July 2020, the diocese published articles on: 'a new neighbourhood centre for Woodley'; 'Thames Valley citizens unite for a more wonderful world'; 'welcoming the Revd Dr Andrea Russell'; 'Clewer initiative launches app designed to eradicate labour exploitation on British farms'; and 'COVID crisis inspires mother and son church bike ride'.

As worthy as all this no doubt was, I was surprised to see these matters being prioritised ahead of the review, and gave up checking the website when the learning review had still not materialised by August.

Then suddenly, without warning, the review was published in October 2020. Steven Buckley even emailed to let me know, but by the time his message had hit my inbox, I had already pored over its thirteen recommendations.

The review was written by Dr Adi Cooper, who had spent twenty-five years in local government as a social worker, manager and director of adult social services, and is the independent chair of two safeguarding adult boards. She is also a visiting professor at the University of Bedfordshire. She had apparently finished her review in April 2020, but COVID-19 and Field's appeal against his sentence – and the legal advice that was subsequently needed – delayed publication.

The review started by calling the case 'extraordinary and unusual', and expressed concern about the elderly and lonely who 'can be made vulnerable by the likes of Ben Field', warning that the Church and wider society needed to be 'ever more vigilant'. The review spoke about the human need for intimacy being universal, and how the Church needed to develop an open and accepting culture as far as homosexuality was concerned. There is even an acknowledgement that the Church of England 'faces challenges to resolve its own positioning on this', as this was 'not conducive to disclosure [of sexuality]'.

However, that was as far as the review was prepared to go. Perhaps inevitably, given Dr Cooper's background and the terms of reference set for the review, the emphasis was on safeguarding policy and practice. None of the thirteen recommendations related to the Church's own doctrinal position about gay Christians – despite an acknowledgement that Peter's sexuality had been the context in which Field was able to groom him. They also admitted that the 'closed culture of the Stowe Church in general, including attitudes towards homosexuality, meant that Peter Farquhar's homosexuality and the relationship between Peter Farquhar and Ben Field was a 'well-known secret', and that it was 'not publicly acknowledged' made Peter vulnerable to exploitation. I was intrigued to read that Dr Cooper had attended a service at Stowe Parish Church in December 2019, although 'all those interviewed or spoken with have been assured that their contributions to this process would remain confidential'. Secrecy was to remain the abiding culture, it seems.

I also couldn't escape the feeling that a more generalised form of victim-blaming was at work, with Stowe Parish Church the most culpable. The church was described as 'evangelical', where being gay was 'deviant and wrong', and against the culture of inclusivity that the review was championing. If this were true, I still question why Peter would have wanted to worship there – but Dr Cooper does not consider that point, nor go beyond a generic statement earlier in the review that this kind of culture was prevalent within the Church of England as a whole.

As I had predicted, the review was keen to see Field as pursuing a 'scam', and to regard the case as 'unique'. While it did concede that there were lessons to be learned, those lessons were of a particular operational type and almost exclusively concentrated on individual Christians, specific congregations and the practice of safeguarding within the diocese. 'Let's all just be a little more tolerant and nicer to each other' seemed to be the core message.

The review did throw light on some of the questions that had previously troubled me, however. For example, it stated that the labelling of Field as a psychopath by Stephen Bushell was not taken any further because he was 'considered to be unqualified to make this professional judgement/diagnosis' – and, critically, no second opinion, from someone who *was* suitably qualified, was ever sought. It also seemed to hit the nail on the head in observing that, as far as the relationship between Peter and Field was concerned, common sense was suspended. Dr Cooper noted that if Peter had formed a relationship with a much younger woman, then questions would have been asked. As the review states, people would have been 'more curious and suspicious ... asking for example "are you sure this is a healthy relationship (considering the age gap)"?' The reason they didn't was 'because of attitudes that parishioners held towards homosexuality, based on a conservative theological interpretation of the Bible, which meant that [Peter's] sexuality and the relationship were not questioned, explored or overtly discussed.'

We might equally apply this judgement to the formal position of the Church of England, as this review only skims the surface of what happened at Stowe Parish Church and how the Church should now respond. Sadly, I was left in no doubt that unless there are more fundamental changes in the formal position of the Anglican Church it will only be a matter of time before we are having to learn even more lessons about other similar cases.

CHAPTER ELEVEN

A Means to an End

'So act that you treat humanity, whether in
your own person or in the person of any other,
always at the same time as an end, never merely
as a means'

IMMANUEL KANT, 1785

I arranged to meet up with Jules again, but this time at
the rugby club rather than in the pub. He'd been in self-
isolation for two weeks after returning from a holiday in
Spain but, pushing through the green gates of the club, he still
looked strangely tanned for the time of year. It was autumn
and, without COVID-19, it would have been the beginning of
the new rugby season. As is now the 'new normal' we didn't
shake hands or hug, but giggled a 'hello' and then, surprising
myself, I gave Jules a quick bow, almost as if we were in Japan
instead of Maids Moreton.

We talked a little about his holiday and then the news that
his eldest son had announced his engagement. As soon as we

started to discuss Jack it sparked off memories for us both of our sons playing in the same team on the very ground where we were now standing, and specific rugby games, and regular rugby tours, became a way of measuring time passing; a way of discussing change, much like farmers might do when they chat about the turning of the seasons and of harvests that have come and gone.

I asked Jules about the time he had played in the same team as both his sons. 'Why was that so important for you?'

'It was like a journey I had been on,' he replied. 'In fact, I kept playing myself just so that I could play in the same team as Jack and Ben. I started at this club when I was thirteen years old, and when my brother was in the First XV. I then played in that team and, even if it was only once, I wanted to play in the same team as my boys. We were in the same rucks, scrums and even in the same fights. It was a special moment when everything seemed to come full circle.'

Jules described how the club really was a community, and I had hoped to end this book with a formal lunch in the club, with all the older members present, sitting around discussing the D-Day landings and rationing, or the swinging sixties, while the 'muddy minis' – eight-year-olds who are just getting introduced to rugby – excitedly chased each other, running between tables and chairs. That had seemed to me like the perfect metaphor for how the various generations can co-exist in the same space and in noisy harmony, and a nice way of concluding a theme that has come to dominate the book.

'It will be some time before we are able to do that again,' said Jules, and then added, 'We can't take any chances before they find a vaccine.'

For a few weeks in August 2020 the club's grounds had become a mobile testing centre for COVID-19. The state's test, track and trace arrangements had formally arrived in Buckingham, even if we did our own informal and interpersonal tracking and tracing all the time.

I had nodded silently about Jules's observation, but he then asked me if I had been in contact with any of the older members, especially 'Tiger' Smith. Tiger is now well into his eighties and seems to embody the culture of the club. A decent player in his youth, he was still running the touchline in his sixties, although he now finds it hard to walk and so keeps score instead. He does that sitting on the bench which celebrates the life of another old boy, who died in 2013, called Rico De Angeli, and he has become such a fixture there that the club has thought it best to erect a rickety wooden and plastic cover to protect him from the wind and rain.

'Yes, I bumped into Tiger in Waitrose,' I replied. 'He was pushing his trolley around, with his mask on his face and, thinking that I was being helpful, I told him that there was no need for him to do his shopping in person as they could always deliver.'

Jules smiled and asked, 'What'd he say to that?'

'Oh,' I said, 'he replied that, "I don't mind getting out of the house at all. It gives me something to do."'

Ironically, for some older people 'shielding' as a form of protection merely served to make them feel even more cut off from society, because they were now also cruelly excluded from their friends and especially from their families. It served to cement their status as alien others, even if it was a strategy that had been designed to protect. Amnesty, which normally produces reports about war zones, thought that sending thousands of older, untested patients into care homes at the start of the pandemic was a violation of their human rights and had 'serious negative consequences for their health and lives'. More than eighteen thousand older people living in care homes in England and Wales have died of COVID-19.

Of course, shielding wasn't intended to be punitive or carceral, but our fear that visiting the elderly in their own homes, or in care homes, might hasten their end only magnified a more common pre-COVID-19 culture of older people's disconnectedness and segregation. Their homes, or the care homes where many elderly people live, quite quickly become prisons. Sadly, for some, it also meant that they died without the comforts that come from being surrounded by loved ones.

As I left Tiger in Waitrose his parting words to me had been 'it won't be long now', and I wasn't sure if he had meant the end of COVID-19, the discovery of a vaccine, the start of a new rugby season, or perhaps death itself.

'He'd probably just have meant the rugby starting up again,' said Jules, smiling, but neither of us would have been surprised if Tiger had been implying his own inevitable demise.

*

If Peter had had some idea that he was facing death, I wondered how he might have managed his awareness of that reality. Are we supposed to rage against death, or meet it with stoicism and fortitude? Philip Larkin, who was always dismissive of religion, was terrified of 'unresting death', and in 'Aubade', his last great poem, he wrote that 'death is no different whined at than withstood'. Christopher Hitchens, one of the world's most famous atheists, faced his own death with an exquisite sense of humour and concentrated his writing in *Mortality* – his final collection of essays, on the process of dying – as much as the 'dullness of death'.

Of course, Larkin and Hitchens had no belief in God, but I do wonder if Peter's faith was a comfort at the end. I'd like to think that it brought him some consolation, but I also get the impression that a number of inter-related issues were preoccupying him towards the end of his life, quite apart from trying to organise his literary and other affairs. In particular, how had he come to terms with his exciting but awful relationship with Field – of his love for him, but his hatred too, as was expressed in their poems, or during their 'rap battles'?

'Exciting' and 'awful' sound oxymoronic in much the same way that it seems to make no sense to both love and hate. However, that's not so unusual. In our unconscious we love and hate simultaneously, and it is only in our conscious lives that we feel compelled to take action; that we feel compelled to choose and take sides. We are all often, and at the same time, pictures of perfect self-control, but also of unseen and irresistible urges. In our unconscious we exist in a state of permanent but hidden contradiction, and it is only our visible and conscious selves that want those contradictions resolved. To quote The Clash, should I stay, or should I go now?

There were attractions in staying for Peter and that, more than anything else, seems to be the most important discovery to emerge from the research I have undertaken. In Freudian terms, Peter's relationship with Field represented his public acknowledgement of his true self, rather than his divided self. He was a gay man who was interested in other men. After he had surrendered himself completely to Field's charms he must have questioned, especially in those first heady and passionate moments, why it had taken him so long to have made that decision. In that respect, perhaps he did also reflect on what a life he had wasted by previously denying himself those comforts.

Of course, Field was a much younger man and I can't imagine that Peter didn't suspect that he was being used. Peter wasn't stupid; he was an intelligent and well-read man. Perhaps he even suspected that the relationship was doomed from the start, but Field's protestations of love and the betrothal ceremony obviously had blinded him to the true nature of their relationship and also ensured his silence when the relationship was clearly going badly.

Formerly cautious about expressing his love, Peter seems to have quickly embraced their relationship, although I accept that this merely raises the question of why he had been so precipitate with Field. Should we blame Peter for what happened to him, like some people in Buckingham were keen to do, conveniently removing themselves from shouldering any responsibility? I really don't think that what happened to Peter was his 'business', by which was implied his 'fault'. Haven't we all done things on the spur of the moment, or against our better judgement, especially when we are in love? I know that I have. And if it had all ended in the normal way, breaking down as many relationships do, I imagine that Peter would have put it all down to experience and the pain of losing his sensual and sexual discoveries with Field would have eventually faded in his memory. No doubt they would have also been replaced. After all, why should Peter have stopped loving simply because his relationship with Field had ended?

Peter would surely have taken comfort from the fact that

he would not have been the first, and nor will he be the last, person to realise that, in the cold light of day, a relationship freely entered into had been hasty and foolish. Over time he would have forgiven himself and chalked it up to experience.

Life goes on, as they say, although tragically in Peter's case it did not.

His relationship with Field was nonetheless important for Peter, for it was about expressing his authentic identity and character; it was about being the person that he had always wanted to be. Giving him agency in this respect is to allow Peter to take control of the life that he wanted to lead and, more importantly, about how that life should be lived. He was not a passive victim, but actively choosing to live in a way that best suited who he was and how he wanted to express himself, with all the messy complications that then came to characterise his life, as indeed they characterise all of our lives – if we are lucky. After all, who wants an uncomplicated life? I really don't think that it is somehow better to live a life that is linear and predictable – an existence that is the equivalent of a straight line. Above all, Peter was no longer having to live a lie and therefore, whether consciously or not, he was challenging the duplicity that seems to be woven into the very fabric of our beings, and especially into the triumvirate of institutions that still dominate Middle England: school, Church and state.

Ironically the individual who seemed to best personify these duplicitous values of Middle England was Field himself. He was proud of being 'vulgarly commercial' and knew only too well which buttons he had to push at UB and in the Church in order to advance. And advance he did, and I have no doubt that he would have gone further – perhaps to the very top.

241

At an institutional and organisation level this duplicity seems to me to be most obvious in the Church of England – not just at the local church that Peter had attended, but, more worryingly, within the doctrinal approach to same-sex relationships. As I have discussed, I did eventually get to read their learning review about Field and his near-ordination training before finishing the book. However, for me, it needed to look far more critically at the Church's own stance on Christians who were homosexual, and how this in turn created the perfect context for Field to operate. The learning review concentrated too much on processes and procedures, rather than questioning the Church's fundamental position about faith and homosexuality.

Field, in that sense, has been allowed to disappear by paradoxically being seen as a 'one off'; unique and exceptional; and as a rare and exotic specimen. That will at least appease his narcissism. But, given this uniqueness, the review seemed to argue, there was nothing about him to trouble their status quo – in this case the everyday workings of the Church. All that needed to be done was to tighten things up a little, and be more welcoming and open.

In many respects the review saw Field as someone similar to Harold Shipman, whose criminal career was treated in much the same way by the medical establishment. Killing over two hundred of his overwhelmingly elderly patients didn't really result in fundamental changes to the organisation of medicine in this country. Instead, the medical establishment tinkered with the issuing of death certificates and tightened up the regulations related to doctors working in singleton practices. Could it stop someone like Shipman killing again? I think not. And that has essentially been the formal reaction to Field from the Church authorities too. Nothing to see here, they seem to be saying; move along now; don't worry.

In the same way that we were asked to take comfort from the fact that most doctors are not murderous serial killers, so too we are in effect being assured that most people wanting to become priests don't have their sights set on killing their parishioners. That's manifestly true, and so perhaps we really should take comfort from that. However, we also need to acknowledge that the likes of Field and Shipman think very carefully about weaknesses in the formal structures and the informal cultures of the institutions and professions they want to join, so they can exploit those weaknesses for their own ends. As a consequence, we should view Shipman and Field as 'black swans'. It's not so important that they are exceptional and unique, but rather the role the very fact of their existence plays in degrading what we know to be true and predictable. So we might know that the vast majority of doctors want to treat the sick and heal them, and that priests want to minister to the faithful. However, the reality of the existence of a Shipman and a Field also means that we have to acknowledge that some doctors and some priests will want to use their medical skills or their religious beliefs for their own selfish ends.

And sadly, sometimes those ends really do include murder.

Even then, Field didn't have an original plot to kill, but stole it from Peter's writing. This was his ultimate betrayal of Peter, but it also shows the limits of his thinking and imagination. Field was not an author, a poet, a Christian or a scholar, but simply an impersonator; a facsimile rather than the real thing, and someone who was prepared to kill to get what he wanted.

*

Death, if we are honest with ourselves, has always been an interesting, if rather hushed, topic of conversation. It has inevitably been one of the dominant themes in this narrative. I might have been dealing with murder, which is of course an unnatural death, but, in the end, the outcome is still the same. As a subject, death somehow draws us close, even if we are never too certain if that is a healthy or a melancholy preoccupation. 'Don't be so morbid,' you'll be chastised if you dare to mention your own mortality. 'You've got years yet,' they'll say, even as we become ever more acutely aware that we are getting up too often in the middle of the night to go for another pee. Too much wine with dinner, we reassure ourselves, and not a symptom of something more serious, or maybe we'll book a doctor's appointment in the morning. Those appointments force us to acknowledge that we are going to die – which is precisely why we don't want to make them.

Is it healthy or morbid to be fascinated by murder? I like to think that what pulls us in is how senseless murder is, and so we are attracted to it as a phenomenon because we want to try to impose meaning on why murder happens. Humans have evolved as a species because they have been able to solve mysteries and problems, and, for me at least, an interest in murder is therefore about trying to make sense where none seems to exist. And if we can make sense of murder – why it happens and who is likely to commit it – then we are in a much better position to do something to stop it happening again. That seems like a noble goal. Perhaps I am merely offering myself consolation here and that an interest in murder really is something to worry about, rather than to take comfort from or defend.

I have also used Peter's murder to consider what it means to be old in our culture, as well as trying to describe the process of dying and the state of being dead. These are all equally difficult issues to discuss, especially as shuffling off this mortal coil is a sensitive subject. There are practical difficulties too. When, for example, do we actually become elderly? I am now in my sixties, but I certainly don't think of myself as old.

This complexity is likely to become more pronounced in the years to come; it has already become complicated during my lifetime. Let me offer a simple example. In 1951 there were 270 centenarians in the UK, but by 2001 there were over six thousand. Latest figures suggest that we currently have more than thirteen thousand people who have reached the age of one hundred. Yet someone who was sixty-five when I was growing up seemed remarkably old and, whispered behind our hands, likely to die within the next few years. My own parents died in their fifties, although that was unusual. It was more common for people – both men and women – to die in their seventies, and very rare for someone to reach their eighties or nineties. Making it to a hundred really was something to celebrate because it was so rare and unexpected.

As this indicates, and as we are constantly being reminded by the media, we are living longer and most of us are living better. However, this biological reality doesn't seem to be accompanied by any sense of joy; it is hardly viewed as a triumph of civilisation, or even as a public good. We may have left behind a life course which was patterned by going to school, finding a job for life and climbing the career ladder before retirement and then death soon after, but historic attitudes to ageing seem to persist. It is still possible to detect a primal fear of growing old, which is often expressed as a fear of the elderly. No one seems to have a good word to say about getting older, and therefore we don't seem to want to acknowledge the progress that has allowed more and more older people to live for longer. Telegrams from the Queen aside, our centenarians are hardly celebrated, partly because Western culture has long thought of being old as lacking in some way – perhaps financially, and certainly in terms of good health; of being disadvantaged; and therefore the elderly are viewed as a cultural and economic burden.

That hardly seems fair.

Most of the culture of being old has been socially constructed. Old age for many people is associated with division and distance. But there is no particular reason why older people have to live in poverty, become religious, be the victims of fraud, theft and – dare I say it – murder. Remember: it is the elderly who are the group most often targeted by serial killers.

None of this is inevitable. It is us who have created the structures and systems which make older people vulnerable and dependent, such as through the inadequacies of the state pension scheme, or employment practices that force older people out of the workplace. This latter point would seem to be crucial, for in an avowedly market economy centred on the productivity and wealth creation of the individual, to no longer be seen to be productive can have serious consequences for how life is experienced by that individual. In short, they are seen to have less value.

Yet being older should still be a time of fulfilment, rather than a period all too often characterised by denigration and marginalisation. COVID-19 has not only caused further physical separation, but it has also highlighted how truly invisible the elderly have become. If we are honest with ourselves, the fact that so many elderly people have died in our care homes hasn't really been a scandal – instead, their deaths were quite quickly silenced by a culture that prioritises the needs of a younger generation and the economy. The elderly have become the human equivalent of collateral damage in our response to the pandemic and so, to push my war metaphor a little further, killed by friendly fire. At some point, there will no doubt be a formal investigation into how the government handled the country's response to the pandemic and perhaps someone will officially say sorry for what happened to our most vulnerable. But by then it will be too late.

*

Death is such a totalising word, that we tend to forget that we need to distinguish between dying, death and the state of being dead. There are further difficulties in discussing all of this as we tend to think of death in the abstract. We think of other people's deaths, rather than our own, because death is something that only happens to other people – people like Peter. We bury our heads in the sand; we file death in the drawer marked 'to think about another day' – but by then, when we remember where we put that thought, it's too late. However, if we again use what happened to Peter as an example, if we want to live an authentic life we need to take charge of our lives, as Peter did, and be fully aware that death is inevitable. In short, we need to decide who we are, and what it is that we want to do. We then need to be who we are, as opposed to what other people expect us to be. Thinking about living our lives in this way allows us to put death in perspective. It is not death that somehow sneaks up behind us and robs us of our life, but we ourselves who do not achieve our potential as human beings during our lifetime by failing to live that good and authentic life. To realise our potential, it seems to me, we must learn to live our lives in this way and, whether we acknowledge it or not, remember that those lives have to come to an end.

Let me use a literary metaphor, which seems appropriate given Peter's interests. If our life is a narrative with a distinct structure and meaning, then it must have an ending. Death is the full stop at the end of a sentence; the final chapter of a book. Viewed like that, death provides the necessary shape that allows us first to view and then to assess the life that has been lived. An unending life would be meaningless for, mixing my metaphors, it would be like a river that never reached the sea.

Death, in other words, is not just necessary, but good for us.

Should we fear being dead – of not existing? Of course, this question is for many people, including Peter, bound up with issues of Heaven and Hell; of unhappy ghosts wandering purgatory; of angels and demons; of 'above and below'. That's not my view of these matters. I am a humanist and so I do not believe in a God, or indeed a Devil. As far as I'm concerned, there is no Heaven and nor is there a Hell – no matter how much I have wanted some of the men I have worked with to go there. I know that murderers, rapists and serial killers cannot go to Hell, because not only does that place not exist, but there is also no such thing as a subjective state of being dead. For me, in much the same way that I did not exist before I was born – a state I neither feared, nor onto which I could project meaning – I will not exist when I am dead. I cannot sing hymns in Heaven or burn in Hell's fires as 'I' am no longer. For me, being dead is simply a state about which nothing can be said or known because we have transcended the limits of empirical enquiry.

My thinking here is obviously secular rather than religious. However, I still attempt to live my life by a moral code, although one derived from reason, as opposed to the dictates of some supreme and unseen being handing down a guide about how to live my life on tablets of stone, and then codified in a holy book. That moral code has been shaped by Western philosophy and especially by the work of Immanuel Kant, the 'little professor of Königsberg' who urged us all to do good, without basing that appeal either on religion, or on the existence of a God who would judge us later, after we had 'passed'. Kant is perhaps our greatest moral theorist and, despite the difficulty and complexity of his writing, he outlines a moral approach to living that is just as important today as it was in the eighteenth century, when he first published his *Critique of Practical Reason*.

More importantly, that moral approach also allows us to think again about Field, and why he came to murder Peter.

*

Now is not the time to discuss why I think that Kant is our greatest Western moral philosopher. What concerns me is Kant's view about morality and how that helps us to understand the murderous relationship between Peter and Field. Kant did not believe that morality stemmed from some supernatural force, but from the innate reason and transcendental freedom of human beings to decide for themselves what is right or wrong, and thereafter how to act upon that reasoning. Kant was interested in finding out what was the best way to be moral. What rules could be brought to bear on how to be good and to do the right thing? Above all, he believed that people should be good not because of what advantages might come to them as a consequence, but because to be good – and to do good – was always right in itself.

The basis of Kant's thinking was the categorical imperative – deriving moral obligations from pure reason. For Kant, to 'act only according to that maxim whereby you can, at the same time, will that it should be a universal law'. In short, it is moral for me to behave in a particular way only if everyone else can do exactly the same thing. This principle of universality is at the heart of the categorical imperative. For example, say I wanted to lie and cheat, or amass a fortune through theft. Stealing might be good for me, but if I applied the principle of universality – if everybody behaved in the same way as I did, and therefore everybody else also stole – would that lead to a good outcome? Clearly the answer is no, and so by universalising our conduct we can begin to determine what is moral, and therefore the right thing to do. So too if everybody lied, then the concept of truth would break down.

The second way that Kant asked us to consider being moral was by thinking about how we treated other people. He said that people should 'act that you treat humanity, whether in your own person or in the person of any other, always at the same time as an end and never merely as a means'. Put simply, to be treated as an end in oneself is to be respected for one's inherent worth as an individual and having equal value to everyone else. That individual is not an object that exists to be used by others, but a rational and autonomous being, with goals, ambitions and aspirations.

On the other hand, we should not use other people as 'mere' means. Of course, we use other people when they serve us a flat white in a coffee shop, or when we have an engineer come to fix the broken boiler at home. However, that isn't using them as 'mere' means, as it requires their consent to be used in this way. Typically, one of the ways to use someone as 'mere' means would be to deceive them by making false promises, or giving them a misleading account of some undertaking in the hope of benefiting yourself. Behaving in this way would be to fail to recognise the other person's inherent worth and dignity; they would be being used as an object with no rights, and so treated as if they had no importance or autonomy.

Part of my admiration for Kant's moral theorising is that it can be used and applied now in our day-to-day lives. Should I behave in a particular way? Well, only if I would want other people to behave in exactly that same way towards me. If I borrowed money from a friend but lied about my intention of paying it back, I would be treating that person as 'mere' means and failing to recognise them as a human being with equal worth to myself. Nor would I want someone to borrow money from me if they promised that they would pay it back but had no intention of ever doing so.

It is relatively easy to see that Field treated Peter as 'mere' means, and not as an end in himself. He consistently deceived him so that he could benefit academically during his studies and also financially by having, in the first instance, somewhere to stay rent-free, and then through what he would inherit after Peter had died. He deceived him about wanting a relationship, and their betrothal ceremony was just another deceit designed to mask Field's true intentions. He also wanted to use Peter's social standing to gain access to other people, both at the university and within the community, especially at Stowe School. As he says in one of his emails, which I have already referred to:

> At the end of term I called Peter and invited myself over. The reasons for this are manifold, but centre on career-minded avarice – I wanted to work at the university (where he was a guest lecturer), or at Stowe school (where he had been head [sic] of English for 21 years.

I can think of no better way than this email to demonstrate how Field used Peter as 'mere' means. He's using Peter for 'career-minded avarice' and, even if he is willing to share his thoughts, which can be inferred by his writing the email, he doesn't share any of this with Peter. He would of course go on to claim that, as Peter lay dying, he told him 'I hated you all along', although, if this is indeed true, it was only stated when it was impossible for Peter to act on what was being said. Nor did Peter ever consent to being used for 'career-minded avarice', but was instead tempted into thinking that Field's interest in him was because he was in love and wanted a relationship. Peter was being played, or seduced if you prefer, but nothing that Field said or did was genuine or authentic. Worse still, he created for himself his own 'Christianity' to justify his actions.

Not only did Field deceive Peter, he also deceived the congregation at Stowe Parish Church and those responsible for ordination training within the Diocese of Oxford. He'd learned the language of religion but not the core message of its teaching. My earlier criticisms of them notwithstanding, those people within the congregation and the Church more generally were also being used as 'mere' means and not as ends in themselves.

Throughout, I have suggested a number of clinical insights that might assist us to better understand Field's personality and, while these are undoubtedly helpful, the simple reality is that he wasn't behaving morally; he wasn't doing good, and nor does he seem to have had the will to do good. None of this seems to have been a consequence of Field being irrational, or incapable of doing good. He also seems to have known the difference between right and wrong, and he was perfectly capable of understanding what constituted good behaviour. Field was sane and had mental capacity. We therefore need to find some way to account for his actions.

For me, he simply seems to have been unwilling to treat other people as ends in themselves, and therefore worthy of respect and dignity. We can think of this clinically as well as a character flaw and label it accordingly, but at the end of the day Field murdered Peter because he viewed him as merely a means to an end, rather than as an end in himself.

For Field, there was no moral truth, only murder. And, in that respect, he was Frankenstein's monster, Tom Ripley and Pinkie Brown, as well as Benjamin Luke Field.

That is as objectively certain as I can be.

*

Jules and I walked over to Rico's bench, where Tiger now sits to keep score. It seemed quite natural for us to sit down to continue our conversation, although quite quickly we stopped talking and simply sat there, looking out at the pitch in quiet contemplation. The seat offered a view that neither of us had seen before. It was a few minutes before the silence was broken, then I heard Jules sigh. I turned to face him and asked him if sitting there, on Rico's bench, made him think about his own mortality.

'Yes,' said Jules. 'When you get into this corner, you do appreciate that you're ageing and that does make you realise that you're not going to live for ever.' Jules paused and then said, 'There will come a time when I'm keeping the score too.'

'Would you want your name on the bench?' I joked.

'No – my name is already up in the clubhouse. That's enough.' Jules paused again and then reflected, 'Maybe Jack and Ben will have kids and they'll want to play rugby too.'

I wondered what he might say next, but then I too became caught up in my own thoughts about getting older. Jules broke the silence by saying, without any hint of embarrassment, 'This has been my life – rugby and my family. And if I have grandchildren and they play rugby, I'll be sitting here watching them too, and I suppose hoping that they'll want to buy me a pint when the match is over.'

He smiled and then we both looked out at the pitch once more.

'That's not such a bad thing to hope for, is it?' I asked of no one in particular.

Jules now seemed totally lost in his own thoughts. I'd like to think he was remembering all the games he had played in, or imagining the ones that were still to come, when he was no longer able to take part, or even to keep the score.

I know that I was.

Final Thoughts with Roger Perkins

Ben Field never did reply to either of the two letters that I sent to him in prison. I couldn't ask him about his time at UB, his grooming of Peter, his faith, literature, the vulnerability of the older people that he had looked after at the Red House Nursing Home and how he had injected himself into the very heart of Middle England at Stowe Parish Church. I couldn't ask if he really would have gone on to kill other elderly people who he had created access to. But then, if I am honest, I probably wouldn't have believed what he said to me anyway.

As I have said, at first I thought that his failure to write back might just have had something to do with the fact he had been given leave to appeal, and therefore it wasn't in his interests to begin a correspondence with me. However I did wonder whether his narcissism would eventually get the better of him, although I certainly never gave him any assurances in my letters about what it was that I was going to write about and, above all, I never implied that by writing to him I was somehow on his side, that the jury in Oxford had made a mistake and I thought he was innocent.

That's an important point to make. The ethics of writing

to people accused, or indeed convicted, of murder have been memorably described by Janet Malcolm in her wonderful book *The Journalist and the Murderer*, which was concerned with the relationship between Jeffrey MacDonald, a convicted murderer, and Joe McGinniss, a writer who seemingly befriended MacDonald but then wrote a scathing book about him and his case. Malcolm uses their situation to warn that journalists who write to murderers are 'a kind of confidence man, preying on people's vanity, ignorance, or loneliness, gaining their trust and betraying them without remorse'.

I hope I avoided her accusations in the letters that I wrote to Field, but there was a cost.

I realised that Field just didn't want to engage with me about the questions I wanted to ask him concerning events in Maids Moreton. Whatever the state of his case, his lack of a response had been predicted by my friend who works as a forensic psychologist and, for different reasons, by Field's old journalism lecturer at UB, Roger Perkins. In one of our earliest meetings at the university, Roger had suggested to me, 'He won't reply to you as he likes to think that he's the cleverest person in the room. That's why he always wanted to get one over on his teachers.'

Roger's comments are of course slightly flattering of me – he's implying that I'd be the cleverest person in the room – and, because Field wouldn't like that, he wouldn't reply. That might be the case but, in many ways, Field's failure to engage with me was not a surprise at all. It really is only on TV, or at the movies, that offenders want to talk all about 'why they done it'. As I have described, in my experience, most murderers are silent and uncommunicative. They never talk about the murders they committed and what might have motivated them to take another person's life. In fact, I would go further and suggest that most of the murderers I have encountered are simply ill-equipped to seriously discuss these issues at all. They lack the insight and understanding, and sometimes even the language, to be able to do so. Only when they decide to engage therapeutically with various professionals while they are in prison, and begin a long process of self-examination, can they genuinely begin to discuss why they took the life of another human being.

That's why my forensic psychologist friend didn't think I would get any sort of reply – there was no information to suggest that Field had wanted to seek out this type of help where he had been incarcerated and, in any event, he'd hardly had time to begin any therapeutic process.

So Field, at least for the moment, must fall into the category of being silent and uncommunicative too. However, I do not think that, like some murderers I have encountered, he is unknowable – in other words, that he is incomprehensible and unfathomable. In fact, he is someone that I recognise only too well from my work, and who seems to me to be motivated by values shared by many others in our culture too: he's vain and self-centred, and so prioritises his own needs above all else. As a consequence, he does not act morally and, in the Kantian sense that I have described, nor does he seem to have the will to do good. I therefore also wonder if Field didn't want to engage with me because to have done so by answering my questions might have prompted him to begin the difficult process of genuine self-reflection and change, and therefore taking responsibility for his actions, rather than blaming others or wallowing in self-pity.

Field has a determinate sentence: there is an end to his punishment, and so one day he will once again be a free man. As such, he can return to Maids Moreton, should he choose to do so, and even restart his PhD at the University of Buckingham. These are just some of the practical consequences that occur after a prison sentence has ended for the person who has been punished by a period of imprisonment. However, there are also more philosophical questions that his eventual freedom and release back into the community would raise. Has he been rehabilitated by the years he has spent inside, so that he will want to do good and behave morally? Will his personality have matured over time? At the moment, these questions seem very difficult to answer but perhaps, should the need arise, Field might indeed say that he has been reformed and that his years in prison have made him a different person from the one who was capable of taking Peter's life. If he was to make this claim, should we believe him? On what basis should we judge any future protestations of reform and transformation that Field might offer?

These questions also highlight an issue that Janet Malcolm never considered in *The Journalist and the Murderer*: to what extent is it the murderer, rather than the journalist, who acts as the 'confidence man' in his dealings with others?

That seems to me to be a fair question to ask and, as far as Field is concerned, there's nothing whatsoever in his background that I can see, or from how he approached living his life more generally in the community, that would suggest we should believe a word he says. Field has shown himself to be the very epitome of the confidence man, skilled at gaining the trust of other people and then betraying them without conscience. He might know how to preach a sermon and deliver a lecture, but nothing that he says is genuine, sincere, or suggests he believes a word that he's saying. It's all for show, rather than offering us an insight into his personality.

So, in conclusion, as I have mentioned my rule of thumb has always been that the best indication of future behaviour is how someone has behaved in the past.

In the same meeting that Roger Perkins suggested Field wouldn't reply to my letters, I also took the opportunity to ask him if he thought that Field was redeemable. 'Could Field ever be rehabilitated?' I asked. Roger looked me firmly in the eye and said:

> I hope that he never is, although I am waiting for the conversion to Islam – his Christian God he will see as having let him down, and so he will want to start again. I'm sure he will use his time to write poetry and he'll become another behind-bars intellectual who pretends that he's learned his lesson.

I think Roger is the sort of journalist that even Janet Malcolm would approve of: no smoke, no mirrors, and no interpretation.

A Guide to Further Reading

As far as I am aware, this is the first book-length account of the murder of Peter Farquhar. However, as I have drawn attention to, there is a radio programme and also a TV documentary about the case: Radio 5 Live's *Killer in the Congregation* and Channel 4's *Catching a Killer: A Diary from the Grave*. Understandably, the case was widely covered in the press, and I consulted a number of newspaper accounts when first building up a broader understanding of the murder and especially how it was reported at the time. The radio programme, TV documentary and these mainstream journalistic pieces remain widely available, but the more specialist print accounts that I found particularly useful were: 'Church to review procedures after murderer was considered for ministry', Madeleine Davies, *Church Times*, 13 August 2019; 'Ben Field the Baptist minister's son who became a calculated and manipulative murderer in Maids Moreton', Sam Dean, *Bucks Herald*, 21 October 2019; and 'Good night, Mr Chips', George Pendle, *Air Mail*, 21 September 2019.

I used Anthony Storr, *Solitude* (London: HarperCollins, 1988) to help me to understand the differences between solitude and loneliness. Storr suggests that solitude is 'necessary for genius', and he also claims that many creative people fail to make 'mature personal relationships'. Throughout the book I mention the cases of Harold Shipman, Kenneth Erskine and, in passing, the murders committed by Patrick Mackay, as well as the phenomenon of serial murder. My own *A History of British Serial Killing* (London: Little, Brown, 2020) – now in its second edition – provides a useful starting point to think more academically about Shipman and other serial killers who targeted older people. For murder more generally, a good overview remains Fiona Brookman, *Understanding Homicide* (London: Sage, 2005).

In Chapters One to Four I consulted the University of Buckingham's website. Also of use was James Tooley (ed.), *Buckingham at 25: Freeing the Universities from State Control* (London: Institute of Economic Affairs, 2001). I used Phillip Brown and Richard Sparks (eds), *Beyond Thatcherism: Social Policy, Politics and Society* (Buckingham: Open University Press, 1989) to help me to describe the philosophy of Thatcherism, and also Eric J. Evans, *Thatcher and Thatcherism* (London: Routledge, 2018). I used the term 'neoliberalism' as a shorthand for opposition to high levels of state intervention in the economy specifically and society more generally, and we can trace the roots of this idea back to Friedrich von Hayek, *The Road to Serfdom* (London: Routledge, 1944). Also see Robert Nozick, *Anarchy, State and Utopia* (Oxford: Blackwell, 1974). The term 'criminal undertaker' was coined by Professor Steve Hall, one the two 'godfathers' of the criminological theoretical paradigm ultra-realism. See, in particular, Hall's *Theorizing Crime & Deviance: A New Perspective* (London: Sage, 2013).

For those sections of the chapter related to Romanticism – the radical and ideological literature produced between 1789 and 1832 – I used: Andrew Sanders, *The Short Oxford History of English Literature* (Oxford: Oxford University Press, 2004); John Sutherland, *A Little History of English Literature* (London: Yale University Press, 2013); Tim Blanning, *The Romantic Revolution: A History* (London: Weidenfeld & Nicolson, 2010); and Jonathan Bate, *Radical Wordsworth: The Poet who Changed the World* (London: HarperCollins, 2020). I rather liked Bate's description of Romanticism as having 'a simultaneous spirit of atavism and progress, of nostalgia and utopianism, of looking back and looking forwards'. I consulted the Penguin Classics (1985) edition of Mary Shelley's *Frankenstein*, a novel which reflects many of these competing interests which Bate describes.

The case of the Canadian murderer Mark Twitchell, who was 'inspired' by the TV series *Dexter*, is usefully explained in Steve Lillebuen, *The Devil's Cinema: The Untold Story Behind Mark Twitchell's Kill Room* (Toronto: McClelland & Stewart, 2012), and other cases that are mentioned can be found in: Scott Bonn, *Why We Love Serial Killers: The Curious Appeal of the World's Most Savage Murderers* (New York: Skyhorse, 2014); and Alzena MacDonald (ed.) (2013) *Murders and Acquisitions: Representations of the Serial Killer in Popular Culture* (London: Bloomsbury, 2013). For the influences on Anders Breivik, see Aage Borchgrevink (trans. Guy Puzey), *A Norwegian Tragedy: Anders Behring Breivik and the Massacre on Utøya* (Cambridge: Polity Press, 2013); Mark S. Hamm, 'The Ethnography of Terror: Timothy McVeigh and the Blue Centerlight of Evil', in Jeff Ferrell and Mark S. Hamm (eds), *Ethnography at the Edge: Crime, Deviance, and Field Research* (Boston: Northeastern University Press, 1998); and David Shields and Shane Salerno, *Salinger* (London: Simon & Schuster, 2013) has a very useful chapter on the number of killers who have cited *The Catcher in the Rye* as their 'inspiration'. The acting career of John Wilkes Booth has most recently been outlined in James Shapiro, *Shakespeare in a Divided America* (London: Faber & Faber, 2020).

A. A. Gill's accounts of Buckingham are quoted in the text of Chapter Four, and his collected pieces can be found in *The Best of A. A. Gill* (London: Weidenfeld & Nicolson, 2017). I mention John Bercow, *Unspeakable: The Autobiography* (London: Weidenfeld & Nicolson, 2020) in the text. Whilst dated, John Clarke, *Book of Buckingham* (Buckingham: Barracuda Books, 1984) provides a more formal history of the town. In passing I mention homophobia: a range of negative attitudes towards people who identify as homosexual and which might include prejudice, fear, discrimination and violence. For an academic account see Byrne Fone, *Homophobia: A History* (New York: Metropolitan Books, 2000) and Gail Mason, *The Spectacle of Violence: Homophobia, Gender and Knowledge* (London: Routledge, 2002).

I refer to David Niven, *The Moon's a Balloon* (London: Hamish Hamilton, 1971) in the text of Chapter Two, as he attended Stowe School. I relied on the school's website for quotes from Old Stoics, www.stowe.co.uk, and for back copies of their school magazine. In passing I mention splitting, and this Freudian concept is usefully explained in Stephen Frosh, *A Brief Introduction to Psychoanalytic Theory* (London: Palgrave Macmillan, 2012). The position adopted by the

Church of England about homosexuality and the associated documents explaining their rationale can be found at www. churchofengland.org.

I listened to Professor Valerie Sanders discuss Harriet Martineau on BBC Radio 4's *In Our Time*, recorded on 8 December 2016. To build an understanding of Patricia Highsmith, who cites Henry James's *The Ambassadors* in *The Talented Mr Ripley*, I turned to Andrew Wilson, *Beautiful Shadow: A Life of Patricia Highsmith* (London: Bloomsbury Publishing, 2010), and mention in the text the three interviews (two of which were on TV) that she gave which I found useful. The Channel 4 *After Dark* interview that she gave in 1988 is especially fascinating, and this particular episode of the series is also covered in Stuart Kelly, *The Minister and the Murderer: A Book of Aftermaths* (London: Granta, 2018), which is a stimulating and challenging account of the life of the Reverend James Nelson. Nelson murdered his mother in 1969, before finding God in prison. I used the Vintage (1999) edition of *The Talented Mr Ripley*.

Later chapters were largely based on primary research. Please see A Note on Sources, but I discuss psychopathy and my use of the P-SCAN in Chapter Eight, and in my own *My Life with Murderers* (London: Little, Brown, 2019). There are a number of accessible books about the subject, including Kent Kiehl, *The Psychopath Whisperer: Inside the Minds of Those Without a Conscience* (London: Oneworld, 2014) and James Fallon, *The Psychopath Inside* (New York: Current, 2013).

I used various online sources about the poet Paul Muldoon, and quote from the *Times Literary Supplement*. I also quote extensively from Ben Field, *For 'Work', Read 'Work': Reading*

Ergodics and Ergodic Reading in Paul Muldoon (Buckingham: University of Buckingham Press, 2014). A copy can be found in UB's library.

For those sections based on *Brighton Rock* I used the Vintage Classics (2004) edition, which has an excellent introduction by J. M. Coetzee. I also consulted Jeremy Lewis, *Shades of Greene: One Generation of an English Family* (London: Vintage, 2011) and Zadie Smith's 'Shades of Greene', *Guardian*, 17 September 2004. Issues about truth are well debated by Julian Baggini in *A Short History of Truth: Consolations for a Post-Truth World* (London: Quercus, 2017).

Mark Seltzer's comment about true crime comes from his *True Crime: Observations on Violence and Modernity* (London: Routledge, 2011). This is a challenging and hugely enjoyable book in which Seltzer, Professor of English Literature at UCLA, observes that 'true crime is one of the popular genres of the pathological public sphere'. He sees in our fascination with this genre a contemporary 'wound culture' that enjoys the spectacle of the torn and private body being made public, so much so that 'on the autopsy table, pornography and forensics meet and fuse'. I also use Stuart Kelly, op. cit., in Chapter Nine as he discusses 'killer clergy', and I was particularly intrigued by his insights that there are no matricides in the Bible; Agatha Christie never used an ordained individual as the murderer in any of her novels; and that there are sixty-six solutions to the board game *Cluedo* in which the Reverend Green will be the murderer.

In Chapter Ten I used Geoffrey Scarre, *Death* (Stocksfield: Acumen Publishing, 2007) and Carl Watkins, *The Undiscovered Country: Journeys Among the Dead* (London: Bodley Head,

2013), as well as Christopher Hitchens, *Mortality* (London: Atlantic, 2012), to sharpen my thinking about death and dying. I found this last book by Hitchens to be particularly interesting and, despite everything that he was going through, warm and funny. I was therefore pleased to read Martin Amis's *Inside Story: A Novel* (London: Jonathan Cape, 2020), in which he writes movingly about his friend's death. He says that Hitchens's last words were 'capitalism ... downfall'. I do so hope that is true.

John Fischer Martin, 'Free Will, Death and Immortality: The Role of Narrative', *Philosophical Papers* 34:3 (2005), 370–403 made me think about the various ways that death has been written about. Not mentioned in the text, I also benefited from reading Richard Holloway, *Waiting for the Last Bus: Reflections on Life and Death* (Edinburgh: Canongate, 2018). The 'last bus' is a wonderful metaphor and death, for Holloway, the former Bishop of Edinburgh, 'brings down the curtain on our moment on the stage, something which we always knew was in the script'. As a Scot, Holloway was no doubt channelling the 'Scottish play' here. In his final soliloquy, Macbeth is all too aware that he is about to die, and observes that:

> Life's but a walking shadow, a poor player,
> That struts and frets his hour upon the stage,
> And then is heard no more. It is a tale
> Told by an idiot, full of sound and fury,
> Signifying nothing.

I also found the more philosophical approach to understanding death by Scarre, op. cit., of great interest and his work influenced my thinking in this chapter. I used Gail Wilson, *Understanding Old Age* (London: Sage, 2000) and Christopher Gilleard and Paul Higgs, *Cultures of Ageing: Self, Citizen and the Body* (Harlow: Pearson, 2000) to gain some broader insight into the various debates about ageing in the UK. There is also reference to Immanuel Kant in this chapter, and for me the best introduction remains Roger Scruton, *Kant* (Oxford: Oxford University Press, 1982). Finally, I discussed Nassim Nicholas Taleb, *The Black Swan: The Impact of the Highly Improbable* (London: Allen Lane, 2007).

Janet Malcolm's *The Journalist and the Murderer* originally started life as a series of articles in the *New Yorker*; they were then collected and published in 1997, with a useful introduction by Ian Jack, by Granta, London.

There are only a few books about rugby that talk about the philosophy of the game, as opposed to recounting famous victories, or the careers of the sport's most talented players. I was therefore delighted to read Ben Mercer, *Fringes: Life on the Edge of Professional Rugby* (self-published, 2019), about a boy from Bath and his career as a poorly paid professional in France. He states that part of rugby's appeal 'has always lain in its inclusivity' – a theme that emerged in my discussions with my friends. For me, this perfectly captures why I love rugby as a sport and why I wanted to end the book with Jules at Buckingham Rugby Club. Coincidentally, before becoming a rugby player Mercer went to university and got a degree in English literature.

A Note on Sources

Broadly speaking, I used three main methods of primary research: interviews with ten people who I thought could bring the story to life, or who could help me to better understand some aspect of the crime; a much greater number of informal interviews; and various online searches related to the main themes of my research. Allied to these three primary research methods I also had access to the Thames Valley Police's files from Operation Naseby that they made available to journalists – which proved to be invaluable in a number of different ways. I have drawn attention to the radio and TV documentaries about the case; Sam Dean of the *Bucks Herald* very kindly provided me with his published court reports about Field's trial. I briefly attended the trial at Oxford Crown Court myself, and Sam was also happy to discuss the case at some length with me. Of course, I have also lived in Buckingham and its environs for the last thirty years. Finally, I employed throughout my research a reflexive diary, which not only allowed me to note verbatim conversations, but also to reflect on what was being said in terms of my own values and interests, and which was therefore helpful in prompting research questions and strategies, especially in the face of 'lockdown'.

My arguments have been built on the information either provided or endorsed by my ten interviewees. The interviews that I conducted were usually face to face, but sometimes also on the telephone (especially during the COVID-19 pandemic) and could easily last for over an hour. The majority of the interviewees were interviewed at least twice, but with one or two individuals, five or six times. I often had to revisit the transcripts of these interviews and check with my interviewees that what was said was accurate, but what we discussed allowed me to build up a number of the themes that came to dominate my narrative. At times these interviews were recorded, but often I simply took notes. My ten interviewees were: Ross Collins; Julian Cook; Mark Glover; Professor Philip Horne; Roger Perkins; Professor Valerie Sanders; and four others who would prefer to remain anonymous, but who all live or work in Buckingham. In the text, I have tended to favour those interviewees whom I could name, although my other interviewees allowed me to triangulate what was being said, or made me think again about the issues which had been discussed.

Valerie Sanders also very kindly sent me copies of the notes that she had taken during the meetings of the Stowe Reading Group that she had attended.

Very little of my interview with Philip Horne appears in the text, as much of my time with him was spent discussing Henry James. Whilst not central to the text, I was particularly keen to pursue with Philip his understanding of *The Ambassadors* and why James did not appear to have been included on the syllabus at UB. Briefly, Philip explained and, later sent me a copy of a talk that he had delivered, in which he argued that James was seeking a fresh, a more open way approaching complicated human situations – he was seeking and finding ways to express the previously inexpressible – the subtle effects of a lie or a secret on the relations of a group, the workings of an uneasy conscience, the gradual process of a character's conversion from one allegiance or judgement to another.

I did discuss with Philip if the 'inexpressible' in James's life was the fact that he was gay. He insisted that there is in fact no hard evidence of this in James's surviving letters, despite what might be claimed by others, and that 'as an artist he simply wanted the freedom to write. He was open-minded and imaginative, but he's not into sex, drugs or alcohol. His passion was art.' Fred Kaplan, James's most recent biographer, says in *Henry James: The Imagination of Genius* that when James looked in a mirror 'he saw a man who had renounced marriage, who had never slept with a woman, and who admired the beauty of men but had no sense that that admiration should ever be expressed physically'. Until he met Field, this seems like a perfect summary for Peter's sexual life too.

I had already shared with Philip that Peter taught a module about modernism at UB, and when we first met I wanted his view about why James had not been included on the syllabus, especially if he was Peter's favourite author. Philip suggested that 'James is difficult; it is an uphill struggle. In a class of about twenty, there would be resistance to reading him and perhaps as few as three or four would get excited. So I don't really blame him for not including James as part of the required reading, especially for undergraduates.' I also shared the names of some of the other authors on the module's reading list. Philip nodded sagely as I named each author and then when I mentioned Greene said, 'Graham Greene wasn't experimental, but he should be taken very seriously. By the way, he was a great fan of James.'

I am extremely grateful for Philip's insight on these matters and it was also Philip who first gave me some understanding of the poet Paul Muldoon.

I used the Hare P-SCAN: Research Version by Robert D. Hare and Hugues Hervé (2001), available at mhs.com – MHS is a leading publisher of scientifically validated assessment tools and is based in North America.

I sent drafts of the book to several of my formal interviewees, and as a result changed a handful of details – mostly about matters that were still seen to be sensitive within the community.

As for my less formal interviews – which easily surpassed fifty – these were often collected as I went about the town on my normal daily business: at the post office, drinking coffee in one of Buckingham's many cafés, or simply shopping at the supermarket. This type of interview afforded me a form of 'temperature taking': they not only allowed me, in other words, to hear what people made of what had happened in Maids Moreton, but also to understand local reaction to specific events such as when Field was convicted, or after the Channel 4 documentary had been shown on TV. Chief among these interviewees was the wonderful Trish Cowley. A number of my local, on-the-hoof interviewees wanted to remain anonymous too, but again I have prioritised within the text those whom I could name.

Outside of these interviews, I also spoke with: Fr Andrew Foreshew-Cain, Peter's spiritual director in London; the author George Pendle, a former student at Stowe School, who was often invited to Maids Moreton for supper; Professor Peter Swaab, an expert on Edward Lear and who therefore helped me to make sense of the 'nonsense' poem 'The Owl and the Pussy-cat'; and Steven Buckley at the Diocese of Oxford.

I have discussed briefly in the text the reluctance of a significant number of my interviewees to be identified, and also the refusal of two individuals to speak with me under any circumstances. Two other people that I would have liked to interview simply did not respond to my email requests, and of course Field did not reply to my letters. Reflecting further on all of this, this seems to have been the product of three related, but different anxieties: first, that Buckingham is a small town and therefore people became worried that they might say something that others would find offensive; a general reluctance to get involved; and finally a desire to put Peter's murder behind them. One or two others had different fears, especially in relation to how speaking out might harm their respective careers, or who claimed for other reasons that these were matters which had to be dealt with in confidence.

I have endeavoured to respect all of these positions, although I have to say that, at times, some of this reasoning seemed like a disingenuous form of special pleading. However, I was not dealing with a wall of silence, but quite the reverse: it was simply a reluctance to be *seen* to have spoken. This was especially apparent when the person claiming that they wanted to remain anonymous was thereafter especially eager to discover what else I had found out. They seemed to want to be involved, but not involved at the same time. I wonder to what extent this is another feature of Middle England or, as I have suggested, a more generalised, widespread and deep-seated cultural fear about discussing death in late modernity.

I have drawn attention to Janet Malcolm's observation in the text that 'every journalist who is not too stupid or too full of himself to notice what is going on knows that what he does is morally indefensible'. I am, of course, not a journalist (although I was sometimes treated as such during the course of my research) and I would argue that there is an extremely serious and morally defensible point to the research I have undertaken: we need to learn from what has happened, so as to prevent similar crimes occurring in the future. I accept that this type of deep personal, community or institutional reflection can be both painful and embarrassing, but I believe that it is necessary if we are sincere in wanting to both understand what happened in Maids Moreton and to make certain that it doesn't happen again. We should not shy away from asking uncomfortable and difficult questions about the stark reality that a dreadful murder really did happen within our community. This was not a particularly gothic episode of *Midsomer Murders* and so we have a responsibility to understand, explain and then learn from Peter's murder.

A number of websites proved helpful as research resources, including those of Stowe School, the University of Buckingham, the Church of England and the Diocese of Oxford. Stowe Parish Church also has a good website where back copies of (most) editions of the parish magazine are available. I have also mentioned the various online resources related to interviews given by Patricia Highsmith; BBC Radio

4's *In Our Time* and a documentary about Henry James presented by Professor John Sutherland. Olney Baptist Church also has a good website, which I was able to consult during my research, but they have since removed the sermon delivered by Ben Field, and so those wishing to read what he said must now consult newspaper archives.

Two of Peter Farquhar's novels – *Between Boy and Man* and *A Bitter Heart* – can still be found at www.authorhouse. com and were also available on Amazon. *A Wide Wide Sea*, which was published by Farquhar Studies Ltd, is now difficult to access, and I relied on a copy temporarily loaned to me. All three books were central in helping me to build my argument. Michael Crick's obituary of Peter was published in the *Guardian* on 18 November 2015. A number of Peter's journal and diary entries have been quoted in the press, and it is possible to see some of these in *Catching a Killer: A Diary from the Grave*. Indeed it was when watching the documentary that I saw Peter had noted in his journal that he had attended his GP on the morning of the day he took his first class at the university, and at which he would encounter Ben Field. As acknowledged, I had more formal access to some of Peter's emails, journals and photographs through the materials made available to me by the Thames Valley Police.

A great deal of my research could be described as ethnography. A basic introduction to this form of research is John Brewer, *Ethnography* (Buckingham: Open University Press, 2000). In essence, this type of research involves the researcher spending significant periods of time within the research setting and gathering materials related to the research question. I think that I can justify my claim to have spent a significant period of time within the place I am describing. At all times I was overt about my research interests and did not seek to hide what I was writing about. Indeed, I was often asked if I *would* write about Peter's murder! Within this overall research process the desire is to prioritise the voices of those who live and work within the research setting and, as a consequence, this is why I have tended to use verbatim quotations – especially from my named interviewees. The ethical dimension to all of my thinking about this type of research is guided by materials found at www.britsoccrim.org. I quote directly from my reflexive diary in several places within the text.

The research started prior to the COVID-19 pandemic and continued during the period of lockdown and thereafter. This did impact the research process in a number of ways. Most obviously, it meant that it was impossible to meet up with people, and several conversations that I would have preferred to have conducted face to face had to be done via telephone or video call. There is no doubt that this subtly changes the dynamics of an interview – it is a two-dimensional experience at best, rather than one that is three-dimensional. Perhaps the best way of describing the difference would be to say that conducting an interview in this way is like watching a game of rugby on TV, as opposed to being at the game, sitting in the stadium and soaking up the atmosphere. There were other impacts too. For example, the Coroner's Office for Buckinghamshire closed, and it therefore took a long time to be given a decision about my request to gain access to the official documentation that was held in relation to the first inquiry into Peter's death. I have also described how the pandemic was cited by the Diocese of Oxford as a reason for the delay in publishing the results of their learning review.

On a more positive note, being in lockdown meant that there were few distractions and therefore that simple practical reality which accompanied the pandemic did afford me more time to write. I hope that the results are not disappointing.

Acknowledgements

I would clearly like to acknowledge all of my interviewees – especially, but not exclusively those interviewees, both formal and informal, who were happy to be identified in the book. Chief among these were Ross Collins, Julian Cook and Roger Perkins. Valerie Sanders and Philip Horne also kindly gave me a great deal of their time, and the benefit of their academic thoughts about English literature outside these interviews. Thames Valley Police – through Mark Glover – were also helpful in making materials available to me. Sam Dean read a draft of the book and spoke with me at some length about Field's court case. I would also like to thank Fr Andrew Foreshew-Cain, Professor Peter Swaab and George Pendle.

At Curtis Brown I would like to thank my literary agent Gordon Wise and my talent agent Jacquie Drewe, both of whom do so much to help, support and guide my writing and media careers. Thank you also Luke Speed. I want to thank Meryl Evans, and at Little, Brown Zoe Gullen and Kirsteen Astor, who skilfully handles all of the publicity related to my writing, and Nicky Crane, who edited the book in such a sympathetic and professional manner, and who even came up with the title. It would be wrong not to also thank the wonderful Rhiannon Smith, and I am very much looking forward to seeing her again soon.

Finally, I want to thank the people of the town of Buckingham for allowing me to become a member of their community all those years ago, and especially everyone at the rugby club, which has been a central part of my life. And, talking about central parts of my life, I became a grandfather in December 2020. Welcome to the world, Cillian.